GoR

Please return / renew by date shown.
You can renew at: **norlink.norfolk.gov.uk**
or by telephone: **0344 800 8006**
Please have your library card & PIN ready.

SUN DAMAGED
—wYm 6/10/2

D0766546

Sixties Boys Unzipped

Alan Hammond

Millstream Books

This book is dedicated to my family and friends,
especially my wife Chris,
who in one way or another have had an influence on my life.

The stories in the book are based on the life, experiences and memories of the author and others. All names of people, places and dates have been changed. Individuals shown in the photographs are not related to any of the story lines.

The band names, 'Modern Edge' and 'Bad Brakes', and the composition 'Suburban Mod' are not meant to represent any particular bands with these names or any song with this title; they are purely names invented for the storyline of this book.

Front cover illustration:
Rocker Gordon Yorke, on the left, with his mate Ollie, photographed at Bristol in 1964. Gordon looks a bit of a lad. (Gordon Yorke collection)

First published in 2011 by Millstream Books, 18 The Tyning, Bath BA2 6AL

Set in Adobe Jensen Pro and printed in Great Britain by Short Run Press Limited, Exeter

This book is printed on paper certified
by the Forest Stewardship Council

Text © Alan Hammond 2011
Front cover photograph © Gordon Yorke
Rear cover photograph © Christine Hammond

ISBN 978 0 948975 94 3

British Library Cataloguing-in-Publication Data:
a catalogue record for this book is available from the British Library

Contents

Foreword *by Marty Wilde*   6
Introduction & Acknowledgments   8

1   The Dream has Started   11
2   Crumpet & Parties   19
3   On Board the *Tirpitz*   25
4   Payback Time   42
5   First Stop Great Yarmouth   49
6   Boils & Nurses at Derby   60
7   On the Road to Manchester   69
8   Trouble in Manchester   77
9   Dodgy Management but the Show Goes On   85
10   From Blackpool to Reading   94
11   A Great Party   103
12   On Tour with the Big Boys   112
13   Football & Showbiz Don't Mix   116
14   Love's in the Air at Reading   121
15   The Worst Week in my Life   133
16   The Sunshine Tour   145
17   The Battle of Hastings   156
18   Back on the Road   163
19   The Dream's Back On   173
20   Could this be our Big Break?   184
21   Back on the Sunshine Tour   198
22   Double Shuffle   214
23   Amsterdam   219
24   All that Glisters is not Gold   228
25   Where do we Go from Here?   231
26   The Fat Lady Sings   237
    Epilogue   245

Foreword

I was 21 when the sixties kicked off one of the most exciting decades in Great Britain's history. I can look back now and see clearly some of the most important things that happened throughout those wonderful ten years.

The sixties were shaped in many ways by the war experiences our parents had gone through in the forties, as I believe they, like millions of other parents, wanted a much calmer and better world for their children. Thus they gave us much more freedom and less discipline than their parents had given them. We were allowed a voice in the way our lives were going to be led, which in turn gave us a much freer, more confident generation of young people who were determined to change their world.

Music was also changing fast after the phenomenal impact which Rock 'n' Roll had had. The new musicians coming through were much more blues orientated than their predecessors and freer thinking too. The Beatles, The Rolling Stones, The Who and The Kinks were just some of the many star names that dominated the record charts around the world – which included America – and suddenly, this little country of ours was without question the musical centre of the pop world.

We also led with our clothing designs, whose styles used to attract millions of teenagers throughout Europe and America, and led us to have major tourist attractions such as Carnaby Street and also that wonderful ladies' shop, Biba, in Kensington, to which my young wife used to make a pilgrimage every other week.

Our country was brimming with confidence as this little island of ours maintained a huge influence around the world in so many different ways. During this period England won the world cup; we also had an amazing air force that gave our country the best protection that any nation could have had; and lastly, we had a thriving car industry which produced Bentleys, Rolls Royces, Aston Martins and even the baby Austin Minis.

I believe these were the best times to have lived in and I cannot foresee them ever being beaten, certainly as far as our country is concerned. 'Long live the sixties' and as a Londoner, all I can say is 'We had the lot, mate'!

Marty Wilde

Introduction & Acknowledgements

First of all I would like thank everyone who bought my previous book *The Sixties Boys*. Was there ever a more exciting time, a more expressive, more sensual decade than the Swinging Sixties?

Sixties Boys Unzipped takes us back again to those days. It was the decade that changed the world and there is romanticism in the idea of having lived through the substantial change in social attitudes of that era, and of course the wonderful music that was around at that time. For me and many others it was a special part of our lives.

I hope you will enjoy this new book; maybe it will just remind you of what a great time it was for us teenagers.

❧ ❧ ❧

Anyone who has written a book knows it's a team effort. My very special thanks go to Marty Wilde for writing the foreword. He is a true icon of the Sixties and is still playing great music to packed houses across the country.

I would sincerely like to thank my wife Christine for all her support, and for her own memories. She has always given me that extra help when needed.

Again it's a great big thank-you to my publisher Tim Graham who has supported me over the years and has published my previous 13 books to a high standard.

Heartfelt thanks go to my best mate, Terry Page, who has jogged my memory about the Sixties and has added his own thoughts and ideas.

My great friend John Clifton has enthusiastically given me some of his own recollections and has been stalwart in checking and editing the manuscript. Grateful thanks go also to Frances Bristow, Sandy Buckle, Roger Curd, Peter Day, Judy Hall and Allan Stanistreet who have all burnt the midnight oil in checking the book.

Special thanks also go to Chris Ross and Tony Green for recalling one or two memories of touring with their bands; they've been a great help. I am also very grateful to Orzella Egan, Pat Mitchell and Stuart Mullins for giving me one or two gems which I have included in this book.

Many others have made important contributions including Ivan and Jill Bluffield, Bob & Wendy Bruton, Dover Saints Scooter Club, Sandra Page, Marc Platten, Ron and Joan Saunders, Stephen Tunnicliffe, Joyce Wilde and Gordon Yorke.

As one or two photographs are from people's private collections a reader may well recognise a photograph that they took themselves. We offer our apologies in advance for not being able to credit you in person.

1967

Dr. Christiaan Barnard performs the first heart transplant.

England football captain Bobby Moore receives an OBE.

The oil tanker 'Torrey Canyon' runs aground near Land's End.

Actor Spencer Tracy dies.

The QE2 is launched by the Queen at Clydebank.

The first statutory breathalyser test is introduced.

Ninety people are killed in a rail crash at Hither Green.

BBC Radio 1 is launched.

Record producer Joe Meek commits suicide at the RGM studio.

Celtic wins the European Cup.

Three US astronauts are killed when their spacecraft catches fire
    on the launch pad.

The bestselling male singer for singles is Engelbert Humperdinck,
    with Sandie Shaw the bestselling female artiste.

The Beatles' manager, Brian Epstein, dies.

27 people die in four days of race riots in Newark, New Jersey.

Che Guevara is executed for inciting a revolution in Bolivia.

Concorde is seen for the first time in public.

The first North Sea gas is pumped ashore at Easington, County
    Durham.

Biafra breaks away from Nigeria.

Singer Otis Redding dies.

The United Kingdom applies for EEC membership.

Elvis Presley marries Priscilla Beaulieu.

The microwave is invented.

Queens Park Rangers are the first Third Division football club
to win the League Cup.

Actress Jayne Mansfield dies.

♫ 1 ♫

The Dream has Started

It's January 1967 and 'Hey Joe' by the Jimi Hendrix Experience is riding high in the charts while poor old Donald Campbell dies when attempting his own water-speed record in Bluebird in the Lake District.

It's said that model Twiggy, the face of 1966, now earns over £10 an hour. That used to be about a week's wages for me, until last week, when our band 'Modern Edge' signed up with a record company. Hopefully, our new record 'Suburban Mod', which we're recording this week, will climb the charts and fulfil our dream of pop stardom and a number one hit. Well, that's the plan, but we'll have to wait and see whether we'll be playing the Hollywood Bowl in America or the Hollywood Bowl dance hall near Birmingham.

I'm about to go out on a bleedin' freezing Tuesday night to meet the other members of the band at our local coffee bar, *La Nero* in Hornchurch. We did a gig last night in a town nicknamed 'God's waiting room' near Brighton, which is twinned with a cemetery in Luxemburg. I'm a bit knackered as we had a great party after the gig with some local girls who were well up for it, and that meant we didn't get back home till late morning.

As I make my way out of our terraced council house in Romford, I say goodbye to mum and dad. He's filling in his Vernon's Football Pools and enjoying a Watneys light ale and an Old Holborn roll-up, while mum, who's wearing her new quilted housecoat, is bottling pickled onions on the kitchen table whilst drinking a Jubilee stout. My younger brother Arthur is supposed to be watching Pinky and Perky on the television in the backroom with his bird Deirdre, more like trying to get his tongue down her throat and his hand up her miniskirt. I scare the shit out of him when I push the door open. I see his grubby little paw come out of her bra a bit quickish. I don't know why he bothers as she's flat as a runway and just as boring. She wears this stupid red beret and has a flick-up hairstyle. The flick-ups are so high it looks like somebody's electrocuted her. Mind you, she has her own Morris 1100. I've never had a bird who owned a car.

Arthur's getting a real cocky little git for an 18-year-old and thinks he's the main face in the house.

As I go out of the front door mum calls out:

'I'm a bit worried about you Nick. You look worn out. You should go and see Dr. Harris; he'll give you a tonic.'

'Okay, mum, I'll do that.'

I'm bleedin' worn out travelling around the country with the band and only getting about two hours sleep a night and meeting lots of girls. Add 20 Woodbines a day and drinking as much beer as I can get down my throat and it can be a bit knackering for a young lad.

As it happens, to keep my mum happy, I did go and see Dr. Harris; he spelt it out that if I continue with this lifestyle I'll have major health problems. A week later Dr. Harris dropped down dead. Mum never said any more after that.

Before I go to the coffee bar, if you didn't meet us previously in *The Sixties Boys*, I'll take you back to 1964 when we first started up our band. It was the year when Mods and Rockers knocked lumps out of each other at Brighton on the May Bank Holiday weekend.

We're all in our late teens and my name is Nick Sheldon. I play lead guitar in the band. My best mate, Steve, plays bass guitar. He now thinks he's a pop star and wears dark glasses. We'll be getting him a Labrador soon and a white stick. Tony's on drums; the birds he pulls aren't the norm – they're odd-balls and have major attitude problems. He seems to attract these. His last one was called Freda; we nicknamed her Fred. She had hobnailed boots and wore a donkey jacket, smoked Senior Service and drank Brown and Mild. Rick's our good-looking singer and keyboard player. He's a pain in the arse and we always end up in the shit when he gets involved with anything.

ð ð ð

There was one other guy who was close to the band called Big Al. He was a mad Rocker and had an even madder dog called Sampson. He looked like a cross between a Doberman and an Alsatian and was vicious. Al was our roadie for a while and always brought the dog with him. Once the dog got to know us we were his best mates. On one occasion it was handy, as he stopped our gear being nicked from our van in the night by biting the thieves to bits. There were other times when we were involved in punch-ups on the road and he gnawed a few arses.

In the end Big Al had to get out of the country a bit sharpish and we didn't get to say a proper goodbye to him. What was funny was that Sampson only ended up being a police dog. There's Big Al running from the law and his best mate is now working for them.

Big Al went over to Australia on the assisted passage scheme which was nicknamed by the Aussies, 'The Ten

Pound Poms'. We still keep in touch and he's now a roadie for a well-known Queensland band.

Our band was on the road for nearly three years and we played all over the UK and Rhodes in Greece. Unfortunately even though we were having a great time, we weren't earning any money. We'd come to the end of the road and decided to pack up in December 1966. So while the Beach Boys with 'Good Vibrations' rode high in the charts, our vibrations were the opposite. Rick's dad – Mr. B as we called him – managed the band for a while, but got himself arrested on fraud and stolen property charges. The not guilty verdict was quite a surprise as he's a bit of a rascal.

My current girlfriend, Diane, who wears the shortest miniskirt in Romford, has a brother called Pete, who worked as a journalist for a music magazine. With his help we went into a studio and recorded a demo disc that Steve and I wrote, called 'Suburban Mod'. We tried to get the vinyl in front of a number of record companies without any joy. We always carried a copy in the gig van in case anybody from a record company came and saw us play. At our last gig in Harwich, a guy came up to us and asked if we'd any vinyl of our band. I gave him a copy of 'Suburban Mod'. I didn't know who he was and at the time I didn't care a monkey's. It was our last gig so we just forgot about it.

A few days later we went out for a ride down the coast in Essex in Steve's motor with a couple of girls. It was too cold for a snog and a grope on the sands, so we sat in the motor listening to one of the pirate radio stations, Radio North Essex. Lo and behold, our record came over the air-waves. The guy we'd given it to turned out to be a DJ on the boat. He thought the record was ace and gave it the big one. He played it two or three times a day for a couple of weeks. He was inundated with calls and letters from listeners asking where they could buy the record. After that, record companies were knocking on our door trying to sign us up.

So we got in touch with Pete, who'd gone to America to work for a big musical magazine. He lined up a record deal for us and got us an agent called Anthony, who was now on the plot, lining up gigs in anticipation of our record making the charts. He was in his thirties with a posh accent and knew the music business, so hopefully we were in good hands.

Rick's dad became our manager once again. He was a shrewd businessman or so we thought. He said he'd taken the contract from the record company to a top solicitor to check it out.

How wrong could we be?

ə﮲ ə﮲ ə﮲

After scraping the ice off the windscreen of my grey Cortina with my mum's wooden spatula, I turn the key and it splutters into action. Before the drive to Hornchurch and *La Nero*, I light up a ciggy and I put on my new eight-track stereo which is playing 'Gimme Some Loving' by The Spencer Davis Group.

On reaching La Nero I'm greeted by Marty Wilde's 'Bad Boy' playing on the AMI jukebox. The other boys in the band are already there having their frothy coffee and chatting up the local talent.

We're having a great night until Rick throws one at us. Rick's one of those guys whose dick rules his brain. He'd previously scored with a couple of girls who worked for a promotion company and they'd arranged a couple of great gigs for us when we were on the road, one of them being in Rhodes. But now he gives a nervous cough and drops his bombshell.

'I've got a major problem, boys.'

When he utters those words the rest of the gang are all ears, including the lovely Diane; Anne, who was going out with Steve; Alec, king of the Essex Mods; and Ronnie, who'd sell his own grandmother for a quid. With one or two other mates we're now waiting for the punchline.

'Well, spit it out Rick,' I say.

'It's like this. You know the two girls who got us the gigs a while back. Well, they've moved to another company and they've got us this fantastic booking.'

'What do you mean?' says Steve, looking alarmed. 'We're committed to our new agent. We can't do any foreigners – that's part of the contract.'

Rick takes a document out of his Harrington jacket; Steve snatches it and has a quick read through. He then lights up a Player's Weights, forgetting to flash the ash to us!

'Tell me this is a giant wind-up, Rick,' says Steve.

'It ain't. After I realised I'd dropped one, I got my mate who works in a solicitors to go through it. He said we're committed to do it, otherwise they'll sue the bollocks off us.'

Steve gets up from his chair, puts a tanner in the jukebox and selects a number. It clicks into action and 'My Ship Is Coming In' by The Walker Brothers comes over loud and clear. Steve then reads the letter out loud. Everyone in the coffee bar is listening.

Our dearest Rick,

It was nice to see you last week. Debra and I both enjoyed our weekend in Southend with you, we must do it again, soon.

We're pleased to confirm that after receiving the signed contract back from you on behalf of Modern Edge, you will present yourselves at Dock 5 at

*Tilbury Docks on the morning of 3rd February
1967 for our Northern Europe cruise on the SS
Good Hope where you will be the headline act on
this wonderful liner.*

*The cruise will finish at Hamburg on 20th
February and as mentioned in the contract you will
have to make your own way back from this port.
The fee you will receive will reflect this and we look
forward to welcoming you aboard our flag ship blah,
blah, blah, love and kisses ...*

Tony, who's pretty laid back, tears into Rick:

'You dickhead, what've you done? Our new record could
be climbing up the charts by then and we're going to be
somewhere on the North Sea in the middle of winter, puking
our ring up.'

'It's good money,' says Rick, half-heartedly.

Having listened to the argument everyone in the coffee
bar starts taking the piss singing 'My Ship Is Coming In'. You
have to laugh otherwise you'd cry. To say we're gutted is an
understatement.

ăν ăν ăν

Thank goodness for Mr. B, Rick's dad. He went to see the
agent and the record company, and somehow sorted it out
for us. He did have a presence about him – over six foot tall
and 18 stone plus, he looked a real handful. He took his twin
brother, Mickey, with him, who was just as mean. The agent
and record company must have thought that Ronnie and
Reggie had come to visit them. The gig on the cruise still had
to be honoured but we escaped any further action from the
company and agent.

Two days later we went into the recording studio to re-record 'Suburban Mod'. The A&R man was Johnny Curtis who spoke all poofy and had a limp, moist hand. He was looking after us on behalf of the company and had some new ideas about how we should record it. We fell out with him straightaway, as he wanted to bring in some session musicians. After telling him to stick it up his arse he had second thoughts. We eventually cut the record and also recorded a B side that Tony had written.

We'd been given some money up front by the company which allowed us to have wages for a good few weeks. Part of the deal was that we had to get some more of our own material put together, hopefully for an EP and an LP at a later date.

On a trip to Tin Pan Alley in Denmark Street in London's West End I got myself a Fender Telecaster guitar and a couple of pedals. While we were up west we went into the 2i's coffee bar, which was squeezed into a basement in Old Compton Street, Soho. There was a great band playing. It's said it was one of the birth places of Rock 'n' Roll. Cliff Richard, Johnny Kidd, Jet Harris and Hank Marvin, my guitar hero, were amongst the many that went there.

When we got back home it was down to business. Rick's dad owned a transport company and had a small empty warehouse we could use. For the next couple of weeks we got our heads down and laid down some tracks to take into the studio. Rick's dad had also got us a Transit van as our previous Commer had gone to that big scrapyard in the sky.

♫ 2 ♫

Crumpet & Parties

In between all the practising for our new tracks, life went on, which meant parties and plenty of crumpet. The band was invited to a party in South Essex by Debbie, well-known on the party circuit. As usual it all kicked off. We'd all pulled and it was going so well. Rick had this bird Nova, a fair piece. She had a sweater dress on which was a bit tight and it certainly showed off all her assets to the full.

Later in the evening Rick disappeared upstairs with her. The rest of the band was giving it the 'March of the Mods' in the lounge with the other party-goers. About 11.00 there was a heavy knock on the front door, Steve opened it. Standing there was a bloke of about 40 who was a big lump and wearing a police uniform under a blue overcoat; he didn't look a happy Dixon of Dock Green.

'I've come to collect Nova, I'm her father,' he said with a growl.

Mr. Diplomat Steve shouted upstairs:

'Rick, have you got your clothes back on yet?'

There was no answer, so he walked up the stairs and shouted out louder:

'Rick, its Nova's old man – he's a copper and he's not very happy.'

After that it was like the Keystone Kops. Nova's dad ran up the stairs like a man possessed. It was a big old Victorian house with four bedrooms and he went charging into each of them. It made him even wilder when he found them all occupied with naked bodies, a strong smell of marijuana and everybody telling him to piss off. Rick had now gone into escape mode and was halfway out of the bedroom window when Nova's dad entered the room. He saw his semi-naked daughter and burst a blood vessel as he rushed to the window to murder Rick. Rick jumped from the window naked and fortunately landed on a raised flower bed which broke his fall. The rest of us rushed outside to watch and take the piss out of him as he sprinted up the road. He looked like George Best jinking up the wing as Nova's old man tried to catch him and kick the shit out of him.

Steve went out with this bird Sue a while back, a right little darling; they were always arguing and made Alf Garnett seem quiet when they went into one. They'd more history between them than the *Magna Carta*. A while back she thought she was up the duff with Steve's baby, but there was doubt about that, as she did share it about a bit. It was a worrying few weeks and fortunately it was a false alarm. On the day when Sue found out she wasn't pregnant anymore, Steve crept back round there like a bad penny thinking the coast was clear. Sue had told her mum the good news, but her dad, a crane driver down the Royal Docks, wasn't home from work, so he didn't know there was no bun in the oven now. He was a real handful and didn't take prisoners. When he came in from work the first person he spotted was Steve. Thinking his lovely daughter was still sprogged up, he grabbed Steve by his neck and said:

'Don't you like rubber, son?'

He was making the point that if he'd used a Johnnie she wouldn't be in the club. He kicked Steve out of the house with his size 12 boots and made it quite clear that his daughter was off limits.

She had now got back in touch with Steve to tell him she was getting engaged to a bloke called Sam out of Barking, the number one Rocker in the area. We later found out he'd a brain as big as a gnat.

Sue had been a Mod, but she'd converted to a Rocker. She was having her engagement party and wanted Steve to go to it. Not a good idea in my book, but Steve was game and he wanted to go. Mind you, he wasn't that brave, because he wanted me to go with him. We are both Mods, so a couple of our Rocker mates lent us these tight jeans and short leather jackets. The jeans were so tight my nuts couldn't breathe. In fact my old man said I looked like John Wayne when I walked.

We knocked on the door, all rockered up, and she opened it. She'd lost a lot of weight and her arse in this tight, short leather skirt was mouth-watering. Steve licked his lips and I knew what he was thinking. He automatically grabbed hold of her and gave her a long lingering snog, which she returned in full. As we walked into the lounge it was full of Rockers as the Dansette record player was pounding out 'Nut Rocker' by B. Bumble and The Stingers. Not a good omen as Sam, this man mountain of a Rocker came over to us; he grunted, gave Steve the evil eye and pulled Sue away. I couldn't believe Sue's mum and dad had gone up the pub and left all this lot to it. I grabbed a tin of Watney's Party Four off the table and poured a couple of pints, lit up a Woodbine and took a sausage on a stick. I looked at Steve as he glanced over to Sue, bending down to pick up her pint, showing an arse-full of red knickers.

'I know what you're thinking, Steve; leave well alone my son, that's big trouble.'

'She looks stunning, Nick, did you see her knockers poking out from that Elvis Presley tee-shirt. Even Elvis has a smile on his face. Why did I pack her in?'

'Hang about; she jacked you in because you gave her best mate one.'

'No you've got that all wrong, Nick, she loved me to bits.'

'If she loved you to bits why did she re-arrange the body-work on your Anglia with a bleedin' claw hammer?'

'I'm not listening to this; I'm going for a jimmy riddle.'

As he disappeared into the bog I looked around to see what crumpet was available. I made eye contact with a girl of about 17 who wasn't a Rocker. She was wearing a tight pair of Levis, a skimpy top and seemed to be on her own. The Dansette started playing 'Rescue Me' by Fontella Bass. I felt a bit energetic so went and asked her for a dance, mind you those tight jeans I was wearing were murder. I hadn't had a piss for five hours as I couldn't get the zip undone, they were so tight. I did the usual and she accepted my invitation for a jive. She kept looking me up and down while we were dancing, especially my crutch area; perhaps the sock I had stuffed down there was showing, it did look a bit bulgy! Then a Gerry and The Pacemakers number came on, 'Don't Let the Sun Catch You Crying', and we had a nice smooch. Her name was Linda and she was wearing my favourite perfume, Wildfire. Love was in the air, then she shouted out really loud as she took my hand off her bum:

'I know who you are now; you're the lead guitarist with that Mod band out of Romford, 'Modern Edge.'

The room came to a standstill when Mod was mentioned. The music stopped and there were more eyes looking at me than at a rabbi eating a bacon sandwich. The Rockers were just about to tear me apart when Linda, seeing the aggro coming my way, said out loud again:

'No its not, he's much better looking than you.'

The Rockers started laughing and put their knuckle dusters away and went back to getting pissed and smoking dope.

'Sorry about that, Nick, I didn't mean to cause you any trouble.'

She seemed concerned, so I played on that. We danced closer and my hand stayed on her bum for a couple more tunes without being pushed away. Then some prick put on 'Tie Me Kangaroo Down Sport' by Rolf Harris, so we crept off to the small box room upstairs and started to enjoy each other's company. It was all going so well when the raging voice of Sam came booming through the house like a foghorn.

'Sue, where are you? Don't you bleedin' hide from me, you've got that wanker Steve with you. He's a dead man if he's with you.'

'Oh no!'

'What's wrong Nick?', said an alarmed Linda. 'I thought we were getting on really well.'

'We were, but trouble is going to kick off any minute now because wherever Sue is my so-called best mate Steve is with her.'

'Oh! It's that type of trouble.'

It was now not only Big Sam shouting out, it was his mates as well and if they couldn't find Sue and Steve, I was the next best thing.

'You'd better leave, Linda, there could be a load of trouble coming my way, and I don't want you getting involved.'

'I'm staying with you.'

I thought that was quite loyal so I had another snog and a fumble, but the shouting wasn't going away, and it would only be a matter of minutes before they came into our room.

Suddenly there was a noise above, a trap door opened and two heads poked out. They looked like Zebedee and Florence from *The Magic Roundabout*.

'Steve, what are you doing up there? There's a posse of Rockers looking for you and Sue.'

Then Sue, with most of her tits on view, said:

'We're back in love, Nick. I don't want to go out with Sam anymore, I love Steve now.'

'That's great timing on your engagement day,' I said.

There was a lot of noise coming from outside our door. Within seconds a grinning Steve slipped a portable ladder down to us. Linda and I went up it as fast as we could. As we closed the hatch door a couple of Rockers burst into the room – we got up there just in time. The loft was massive; her dad had set up a model railway track all around it. There was also a settee still warm from Steve and Sue's activities. Nearby a pair of red lacy knickers was hanging from one of the signal arms on the track.

'Well, Steve, what happens now, any ideas?'

'It wasn't meant to happen like this, Nick.'

'It never is with you; we always end up on the buffers!'

We both looked at each other and started giggling.

'I like that,' said Steve.

The long and short of it all is that the girls went down the ladder and gave Sam some cock and bull story about why he couldn't find them. After that, the natives went back to partying and we played trains till the coast was clear. Once the Rockers had left the house we caught the milk train back home.

In the end Sue decided to stay engaged to Sam, when Steve said he couldn't commit to her long-term. The longest he'd gone out with a girl was three weeks, so she'd no chance.

♪ 3 ♪

On Board the *Tirpitz*

We're now going from trains to boats and it's the day of the cruise. It was quite a sad day as the renowned record producer and songwriter Joe Meek had committed suicide. He had an impact on many early sixties bands including The Tornados with their hit 'Telstar'. His death came eight years to the day after Buddy Holly died in that air crash.

It was snowing hard as we made our way to Tilbury to catch the boat. Rick's dad drove us in his brand new Jag. All we had to take were our guitars as the boat had all the necessary musical gear on board. We put Radio Caroline on and they were playing 'Friday On My Mind' by the Easybeats. This was a great number and we made a note to include it in our sets. Hopefully they'd be playing our record soon on this station.

As we made our way through the snow to Dock 5 we could see a grey mass on the water line in front of us. I was saying to myself please don't tell me that this is the SS *Good Hope*. Then Tony who's a bit of a World War Two enthusiast said,

'I thought they'd sunk the feckin' *Tirpitz*.'

'Are they gun turrets up there on the left?' says Steve.

Rick gave a nervous laugh as we got nearer and could see the name of SS *Good Hope* on the side of the boat. Steve was not a good sailor and it didn't help that his granddad was torpedoed in the North Sea during the war. He'd got the right arse ache and said:

'I'll tell you what, Rick, this ain't funny; this boat looks more like 'No Hope' than 'Good Hope'. It's a rust bucket and it looks like it could easily sink in a bleedin' gale, it makes the Titanic look seaworthy.' As he was saying this Barry McGuire's record 'Eve Of Destruction' came on the radio and we all burst out laughing.

We got all the paperwork sorted out and the cases were loaded on board. I was the last one of the band up the gangway. It had quite a steep slope and in front of me was an old couple struggling to get up there; the old man had a bad limp. I dropped my passport which fell down a few steps. As I was picking it up I heard this metallic clanking noise coming my way. I looked up the stairs and this feckin' metal thing was hurtling down towards me like a torpedo. It hit my leg and blood started oozing out of the bottom of my brand new John Collier flares. The pain was horrendous and I was lying at the bottom of the gangway in a daze asking myself 'what the bleedin' hell's happened here?'

Within a few minutes I was in an ambulance being carted off to hospital where they put four stitches in my leg. It was then a mad rush back by taxi to get me back on the boat before it sailed. Now you won't believe this, the metal thing was the old boy's artificial leg; it had come adrift and scored a direct hit on my leg. Well the piss-taking after that from the band was cruel. They nicknamed me Douglas Bader.

I was sharing a cabin with Steve. It was so small that when you walked in you couldn't turn, so you walked out backwards. If this was the star billing accommodation, what was the rest of it like? We took our clothes out of our cases and hung them up in the small wardrobe. Steve sniffed and said:

'What's that evil bleedin' smell?'

I was embarrassed; my mum had packed my clothes with mothballs.

We had bunk beds in the cabin, so we tossed a coin and I got the bottom bunk. That meant I would be bombarded with farts all night.

Tirpitz sailed out of Tilbury into the driving snow. We went outside to wave to the onlookers. There weren't any. It was as cold as a penguin's bollocks on deck, so we headed for the bar. We weren't playing tonight so we could suss out the battleship.

The entertainment manager, Leslie, made himself known to us; he was wearing a wig which was a joke. It looked like a cowpat on top of his head. He was a teapot, so you made sure he was in front of you and not behind. The boat was made up of geriatrics, and more geriatrics. Then a glimmer of hope, there was a large party of students on board, so that could be interesting.

Within an hour the boat was rocking and rolling and the band was puking for Britain. I've never been so sick in all my life.

⸙ ⸙ ⸙

The first port of call was Bergen in Norway, where they say it rains over 300 days a year. After a Woodbine breakfast, Steve, Tony and I made for the ballroom where we were playing that evening. None of us could face food after being Tom and Dick all night. Rick hadn't shown yet, which was good news for him as the way we felt we'd throw him overboard. The so-called ballroom was a dump, the amps were prehistoric, the microphones were useless and the little toy drum kit was a joke.

Leslie came over to us and had a word. He was about 50 and had now taken his syrup off. He wore black-rimmed glasses and this over-sized jacket and white trousers. He looked like Sergeant Bilko in the Phil Silvers show.

'What do you think, lads? Lots of stars have played this marvellous venue.'

'Any of them still alive?' remarked a sarcastic Tony.

'I have to say, Leslie, this must be the most dismal place on earth; in fact I'm expecting to see Glenn Miller and his band come on stage in a minute.'

'It's not that bad, Nick.'

I was just going to slag him off when from the corner of my eye I saw this goddess enter the ballroom. She was late twenties, with natural blonde hair that made Britt Ekland look average. Who was with her but our singer, tricky Ricky, looking like a film star. He'd really scrubbed up well, even for him. Unfortunately for the other members of the band he's really good looking, and has a smile that has all the girls drooling. He also has a great voice. It makes us feel inadequate. He swaggered over to us with an air of 'look what I've just pulled' and said:

'Can I introduce Sigrid from Norway, our cruise director.'

'You on the staff now then, Rick?' said a sneering Steve.

'Hello boys,' she said. There was sex oozing from her voice, we all got an instant hard on.

Rick was standing there, full of himself. Suddenly *Tirpitz* went on a roll, Rick was caught off balance and fell arse over tit into the orchestra pit. Sigrid rushed down to pull him out while we all took the piss. After order was restored Sigrid said:

'I'm looking forward to hearing you play, boys. Should be a really good night.'

ॐ ॐ ॐ

Tirpitz must have found a quiet spot on the North Sea as we went in to have some nosh in the restaurant. They'd tried to put us below the waterline to eat with the troops; we were having none of that, so we went straight up to the Ocean Restaurant with the customers. I have to say the food was tip-top, and it was also our first opportunity to view the young ladies on board.

The talent on show looked promising, there were about 200 students aged 16 upwards, mostly girls. They came from a number of grammar schools in Kent, so we were reliably informed by Rick, who of course had the inside info from his Norwegian bird. Rick didn't join us; he said he was seeing Sigrid and she had a nice surprise for him.

We had two shows each evening for six nights. The rest of the time was ours to do whatever we wanted. There was a bit of good news, a call to the ship had come through from Rick's dad to say our record was being launched tomorrow. He also mentioned that the music press had given it a good review.

We had our own steward who looked after our cabin, a nice old boy called Raj. He was proud of his heritage and religion, and he didn't like swearing. He bollocked me for calling Steve a wanker after he'd nicked my last sherbet lemon. Later I wondered how he knew what the word meant.

We also cottoned on that we could use room service without paying for it. We would order it, walk a couple of cabins up and give them the number of the cabin we'd stopped at. As the trolley of food was being brought down the corridor by the steward, we would stand outside this cabin like it was ours. We would sign for it, and when the steward walked away we would then take it to our own cabin.

Just before the first show we ordered a load of food. As we were stuffing our faces Raj entered our cabin to tidy up.

With too much to eat I said to Raj:

'Are you peckish?'

'How many more times have I got to tell you, I'm Hindustani?'

∂∾ ∂∾ ∂∾

Steve and I knocked on Tony's cabin door to go to the gig. Tony came out with so much Tru-Gel on his nut, it looked like an oil slick.

'You've overdone that my son, I think you've put the whole 2/9d tube on in one hit,' I commented.

'Who's asking you? At least I don't put gallons of that Old Spice on like you.'

Normally when Tony has got the arse ache his Farmer Giles are playing up. So we didn't wind him up anymore, until Steve said two seconds later:

'I'll tell you what Tone, don't light up a fag near your hair or you'll go up in smoke.'

We reached the ballroom and went into our dressing room, also known as the green room. Rick was late as usual, so the three of us had a quick sound check. The large stage had a curtain across and I had a peep through to see how many people were coming in. There were more wheelchairs out there than at Frinton-on-Sea. The average age looked about 90. We were going to open with 'Substitute' by The Who. Looking at this lot it should be Tom Jones's 'Green, Green Grass of Home'. I called Steve and Tony to check out the audience.

'What're we doing here, lads?' said Tony. 'This trip's a joke.'

'You can say that again, we've got a record coming out tomorrow and we're playing to a load of wrinklies who look more dead than alive,' says Steve. 'And by the way where's that mental defective who put us here?'

'Hang about,' says Tony, 'that blonde Norwegian's coming our way with a prat in a white suit and bald head. He looks like an ice cream salesman.'

We went back to the dressing room to get ready. Sigrid breezed in with him; he looked nervous and went to the back of the room. On closer inspection he had a large gold earring in his right ear.

'Are you ready to party,' said an excited Sigrid.

'Well, yeah, when lover boy turns up,' I said.

There was a shuffle and the ice cream salesman said:

'I'm here, I thought I'd surprise you lot. This is my new look, cool ain't' it?'

To say we were gobsmacked was an understatement. We just couldn't take it on board. Here we were, a Mod band, about to take the charts by storm and our lead singer looks like a bleedin' advert for Omo. We were just about to throttle him when the buzzer went and we had to go on stage.

We played the Who number, then went straight into 'Paperback Writer' by The Beatles. After that, the whole set of an hour was chaos. We couldn't take our eyes off Rick who pranced about the stage like a demented chicken. Because we were looking at him, we couldn't play a note. It didn't matter, as the audience of grey-haired old codgers went for their cocoa well before the finish. When the last note was struck there were only two people left on the ballroom floor. One had been dancing on her own all night. She had the biggest arse I've ever seen; she could crack hazelnuts in her cheeks. The other person left was an old boy with a tartan hat and wearing a kilt, pissed out of his brain. He came on stage and kept trying to sing 'I belong to Glasgow' whilst trying to do the splits. This wasn't a pretty sight as he'd nothing on under his kilt. When we got back to the dressing room it was manic. First Sigrid came storming in followed by Leslie a.k.a. Sergeant Bilko. She went mad and tore into Rick.

'Before we booked you through head office, it was agreed by you, Rick, that you could play a more melodic type of music for our elderly clientele.'

Steve took the piss and said:

'He can't even spell it, let alone play it.'

'Who's talking to you, son, you can hardly see in those ridiculous dark glasses?'

I had to laugh, that was the first time I'd seen Steve lost for words. Then Bilko had a pot at Rick. It was all kicking off. Then it got personal and she said:

'You look stupid with a bald head, earring and white suit.'

'You said I looked cool,' says Rick. 'It was your idea.'

She stormed out of the room followed by Bilko. For a second I felt sorry for Rick.

'I suppose you think I'm a bit of a donut,' said Rick, looking for a sympathy vote.

'It's the same old Rick, dick over brain,' said a not very sympathetic Tony.

৵ ৵ ৵

If the first set was crap, the second set was out of this world. There were plenty of girls on show. The students and the other young people on board were up for partying. There were about six birds to one bloke.

We played all our own material plus a few numbers like 'Whatcha Gonna Do About It?' by The Small Faces. Of course when it's going well all the band is giving it the big one.

While you're playing you're looking out for a couple of girls for after the gig. Steve and I hunt in pairs and always stand next to each other on stage.

When it comes to girls we're telepathic and we both know what each other is thinking. Halfway through the set Steve looks at me and nods over to a couple of girls who are dancing near the front of the stage. They keep smiling towards us; we know it isn't for the bald-headed penguin doubling as our singer. Mind you he does have one fan as Bilko comes into the ballroom in this ridiculous red suit and white shoes. He keeps smiling towards Rick. When we stop for a change of guitars I whisper in his ear that Bilko's on the plot and keeps looking at his arse. Rick goes bleedin' loopy and would've killed me there and then if it wasn't for the appearance of Sigrid in a low-cut, blue dress. You can never understand a woman can you? An hour ago Rick was dead meat and now she's fluttering her eyelashes at him.

ay ay ay

We have a ten-minute break; Steve and I jump off the stage and go over to these two girls. They're from Ramsgate and are about 17. There's definitely a bit of chemistry between us. I go for the dark-haired girl called Pamela. She has these long red and white striped knee-length socks and a white miniskirt. Her top is a buttoned-down shirt with epaulettes and a thin, loose-hanging, red tie. With her Evening in Paris perfume and the pink lipstick on her pouting lips, I'm now in love mode. For the first time ever Steve is not arguing the toss who should have who. The other girl is Sheila, who seems nice especially as she doesn't have a bra on. We make arrangements to see them after the show.

We finish the last number and go over to the girls. After the small talk, it's time for Steve and me to get to know them a bit better. Of course there's a problem. You can't go out on deck unless you want pneumonia, our room's too small and I certainly don't want to see and hear Steve rogering away above me on the top bunk all-night. As we're about to go for plan B, their room, it is all taken away from us. We're just leaving the bar when the MPs come out of nowhere. The guardians of the students are on round-up time, gathering their flock from all parts of the boat. There are four old maids in their fifties, you know the type, short hair, tweed suits, no makeup and look like they've never had a good seeing to. As the girls are being marched away Pamela shouts out:

'Sorry, Nick, see you both at breakfast tomorrow.'

That's that, the Military Police have won tonight, but there's always tomorrow. We're at a loose end now, so after a few more beers Steve says with a cheeky grin:

'Let's have a laugh, follow me.'

He takes us to the top deck, stops outside a cabin and says:

'A lot of people leave their breakfast card on the door knob with their requirements. Take this cabin, for instance, they want the full English breakfast which includes one sausage.'

'What're you on about, Steve?'

'Shall we change the one sausage to four?'

He then alters the card to four.

'You little toe rag we can't do that – can we?'

For the next hour we alter loads of these cards all over the boat. The final one is Tony's. He likes to have his breakfast in his room now. He's a greedy bastard and he does like a sausage. He's put four down on his card so we alter it to fourteen.

৯ ৯ ৯

Steve and I went down for breakfast next morning and everybody was complaining there were no sausages; we just grinned at each other. Pamela and Sheila joined us for breakfast and promised that they would make it up to us tonight. They were clearly embarrassed about going to bed early last night.

Today was a special day, my 20th birthday. You wouldn't have thought so, as the only person who gave me a card was my mum who had put it in the case for me to open; it smelt of moth-balls. Tony joined us at the table, looking a bit uncomfortable.

'What's wrong, Tone?'

'Do you know they gave me 14 sausages for my breakfast this morning?'

'You didn't eat them all, surely,' says Steve sniggering.

'Of course I did, I do like a sausage.'

We told the girls what we'd done last night and we all burst out laughing.

'What's funny about a sausage,' says Tony. 'Oh, by the way Nick, happy birthday today.'

He gave me a card and a present.

'This is from the band and as we're at Bergen today you can buy the beers.'

I was well chuffed that they'd remembered as I undid my present. Rick joined us and took some terrible stick about his bald head.

I opened the present; it was a union jack guitar strap with a matching pick. As it happens it was a nice strap and would go well on my Fender. Steve gave me a book, Bert Weedon's *How to Play a Guitar*! As soon as Pamela knew it was my birthday she whispered in my ear:

'I haven't got a birthday card Nick, but I can give you a nice present later!'

It looked like it was going to be a good day in one way or another. In fact it was so good that Bergen had its first day without rain in three months, and the sun started to shine as we got off the *Tirpitz*.

The band, with Pamela, Sheila, Sigrid and Tony's girl, Jill, who was a hairdresser on board, headed for a bar that Sigrid knew. Tony's girl seemed a fair sort. The only thing, she was a bit on the tall side and she had a fair pair of noshers. In fact she could change a light bulb in a twelve-foot high room with them.

Bergen is surrounded by mountains and has one of the largest ports in Europe; it's also a bit on the expensive side as I was going to find out.

As soon as we stepped into the bar, the owner Kurt was all over Sigrid, he was in his late twenties and wearing one of those colourful Norwegian fleeces, which you wouldn't be seen dead in. They'd lived in the same village when they were younger and were good friends. The bar was decked on a musical theme, and they'd pictures of all the latest sixties pop stars on the wall, but not us I'm afraid.

Music was playing from a radio and they must have had a resident band playing there, as there was a small stage with some amps and a drum kit on it. As it was my birthday I got the first round in. When Kurt said how many kroner it was I thought he was taking the piss. The round came to more than I was earning on the *Tirpitz*. I thought any moment Bob Monkhouse would appear and I'd be on 'Candid Camera' as wally of the week. I'll tell you what I've never seen so many people sip their drinks so slowly, knowing that one of them was going to have to buy the next round. So I made sure I finished my lager quickly. I was looking around at who was going to buy the birthday boy a drink when out of the blue our record came over the airwaves. We looked at the radio, then at each other and listened to it in amazement. What a buzz having your record played in a foreign country, bearing in mind it'd only been out a day. After it finished the DJ said a few words and then 'Sunny Afternoon' by The Kinks came on. Our girls were well impressed; Pamela smiled, then looked at me, winked and said:

'I can't wait for tonight.'

'Nor can I,' I replied.

Once Kurt knew it was us on the radio, he was star struck.

'What did the DJ say about it, Kurt?' Steve asked.

'He thought it was a great record.'

After that, drinks were on the house, courtesy of Kurt. There was a catch; he wanted us to play in his bar. Of course with free booze and fresh Norwegian salmon sandwiches made by his gorgeous wife, Kirstin, how could we refuse his request? He fetched the guitars and mics from a room at the back of the bar and we plugged in. What a party we had. The Bergen grapevine quickly attracted more punters and within a few minutes the bar was heaving, it even spilled out into the street. Everybody was dancing and having a great time. We just about managed to get back on board before the boat sailed.

ﻬ ﻬ ﻬ

Tonight all Steve and I have on our minds are Pamela and Sheila. I'm hoping for a birthday present to remember. We go into one of the bars and the girls turn up looking quite delightful in their short skirts and tight tops. The idea is that we'll leave the bar early before the military police turn up looking for the girls. We decide to go back to our room in two shifts. Before we came out we'd tossed a coin to see who would go first. Steve tossed a penny and called heads. Heads it was, so he's going to take Sheila into our room first. He always seems to win the toss; I later find out he's got this two-headed penny off Ronnie. It's agreed that he won't spend more than 45 minutes in our room. They shoot off while Pamela and I have another drink. We try to go back to her room, but the military police have sentries on duty to stop randy blokes like me, so that's not a starter. I check my Timex watch and Steve is well over his allotted time so we make our way to my room. We see Raj in the corridor, he looks a worried man.

'Mr. Sheldon, I don't know what's happening in your room, it sounds like your friend has a herd of horses in there.'

'That's about right; he does gallop along when he's in full flow.'

Pam and I burst out laughing as we make our way to the cabin. I don't know about horses, it's more like a whole stable is in there. I shout out and knock on the door:

'Come on, Steve, the gallop's over.'

He's having none of it and it sounds like he's going over Bechers Brook. I'm just about to unlock the door when there's an almighty crash and Sheila starts screaming. I open the door and all I can see are two bare arses in the air. Steve's bunk bed has collapsed on to mine. Now I know why they call it a bunk-up! What a mess. Pam and I roar with laughter. The two of them are scrambling to put their clothes back on while I take the piss out of Steve.

'It looks like that jump has come to nothing my son. You will go that extra mile, Steve; you know you're much better on the flat than the hurdles.'

'What's your name – Peter O'Sullivan?'

Suddenly Raj enters the room; he immediately clocks the semi-naked bodies and puts both hands over his eyes, but I see him make a gap between his fingers as Sheila is putting her blue bra back on over a fair pair of knockers, the little scallywag.

ଈ ଈ ଈ

Mr. B put a call through to the *Tirpitz* again; our record was getting more great reviews from the music industry and they wanted us back as a matter of urgency. The record company and the agent struck a deal with the cruise company and agreed that we'd get off at Stavanger to catch a plane and they'd replace us with another band. Our agent had booked us a UK tour to promote the record. The first gig was in four days time in Great Yarmouth. So it was goodbye to everybody on board *Tirpitz*.

There were a couple of good laughs before we left. Steve had seen this shirt in the shop on deck three. The bloke who was serving was an Italian. Steve asked him how much it was and was there any deal going, but he didn't seem to understand Steve's cockney accent. After a bit of bartering the Italian stuck his two hands up indicating ten bob. Unfortunately on his left hand his little finger was missing. Quick as a flash, Steve, the wicked bastard, said:

'Nine bob then, mate.'

I know you shouldn't laugh at somebody who's lost a finger, but I rolled up.

Another giggle was when we were nearing Stavanger; we went out onto one of the decks and got talking to one of the crew who said they called the deck we were standing on 'Death Row'. The reason was that on the long winter cruises they'd found dead passengers frozen on the deck. We thought he was winding us up, but it was true, they'd go on deck for a bit of fresh air, sit in one of the chairs and not wake up.

We couldn't resist one final laugh. We decided to have a haircut on board before we left the boat, all except Rick who was now trying different potions to make his hair grow quickly. We thought we'd have a laugh on Tony. As mentioned he suffers with his Farmer Giles, in other words piles. The gel he uses is similar to his tube of Tru-Gel. He also has a small bald patch which you don't talk about otherwise you get a drum stick where the sun doesn't shine.

We were in the salon watching Tony have his haircut done by his bird, Jill. He'd brought along his Tru-Gel, he only ever puts that on his hair. But what he didn't know is that we'd swapped this for his pile ointment. Jill had finished the cut and without looking at the tube started to rub this ointment into his hair. She really had to work it in. Tony was really enjoying it and had his eyes closed. You could tell that, as the sheet that was wrapped around him had now risen considerably. We were pissing ourselves with laughter as she was having a real job putting this stuff on. When she'd finished, all his hair was standing up and it had a real sheen on it. With it standing up it looked like he hadn't had it cut. Tony's face was a picture when he opened his eyes and looked in the mirror. He couldn't believe what he was looking at. Then we started:

'I tell you what, Tone,' says Steve, 'that Tru-Gel makes you look like you've got piles of hair.'

'Why is your hair piled up like that?' I said.

Tony then started scratching his head.

'I thought that stuff stopped the itching,' sniggered Steve.

We couldn't hold it in anymore and fell about laughing. Then the penny dropped as Tony jumped out of the chair and grabbed the Tru-Gel packet. We were out of that room in seconds.

We left the *Tirpitz* after saying farewell to Sheila and Pam. There were tears from Sigrid and Jill as Rick and Tony said their goodbyes. We left for Stavanger airport and were now heading for Luton.

♪ 4 ♪

———— • ————

Payback Time

We had a two-day break before the start of our UK tour. Our record had crept into the top 50 and we were hoping it would make the top 20. Half the gigs we'd be playing on our own and the other half we were lined up with two well-known bands, a challenge for us, as they were chart-topping groups.

I saw my girlfriend Diana and it was agreed that we'd go our separate ways, but still be good friends. To be fair I wasn't much of a catch because there's no way I was going to be faithful, as I hadn't been on the *Tirpitz*. She'd already said that she was seeing other blokes while I was away, so that suited both of us. I still fancied her big time and asked her if she wanted one last night of passion; she declined my invitation with two words, the last word being 'off'!

My brother Arthur had qualified as a chef and got himself a job in a hotel in Southend. He'd only been there a week and there was an outbreak of food poisoning – no wonder, he never washes his hands. My dad was still working at the brewery in Dagenham and sherbeting it up with his mates down the British Legion every night. Mum hadn't been so good; she was under the hospital at the moment. She didn't complain, but I was a bit worried about her. She was a great mum; you only have one mum so she was very special. While I was away, Nobby our cat, a good name for him, died of a heart attack; no wonder, he must have shagged most of the cats in Romford.

&❧ &❧ &❧

On the last night before the tour we went to our local pub, The Queen's Arms, run by Larry. When we were kids, Steve and I would take empty beer bottles back to the off-licence in the Queen's to claim the penny a bottle, the going rate on returns. The previous publican, Fred, would give us the money and everybody was happy. A couple of hours before the brewery came to pick up the empties Fred would put them in crates behind the pub. When the coast was clear we'd nick a couple of crates. Next day we'd take the bottles out of the crates and drip feed them back to Fred to claim our money; he was none the wiser. It worked so well we went further afield to other pubs around Hornchurch and Romford. In fact we made ourselves a couple of carts and pulled them behind our pushbikes.

When you first started smoking as a kid you'd start with cheap Anchor Tipped or Weights. We didn't, as we were coining it in; we started off with Senior Service or Capstan Full Strength. On the chocolate front we'd buy Crunchies, Munchies, Galaxys and drink gallons of Vimto; it was Christmas every day. Of course it couldn't last. We got stopped by the Old Bill as we were cycling down the London Road in Romford. The coppers said we had more beer crates on our carts than the drays coming out of the local brewery.

We walked into the Queen's and Larry took the piss, shouting out to everybody in the pub:

'Hold tight, here come our pop stars, Lulu and Cilla.'

We ordered our pints of Red Barrel and Steve flashed the ash with these king-size Peter Stuyvesant fags. It was a wonder he could see to light his fag up with his Zippo lighter. He'd got these new gold-rimmed dark glasses on and looked like Stevie Wonder; pity he couldn't sing like him. After a couple of gulps of beer I called Larry over to our table. His eighteen-stone frame, clutching a large scotch, waddled over to us.

'What do you two want?'

'I bet your water rates are high?'

'What're you on about, Nick.'

'There's more water in this pint of Red Barrel than there is in the bleedin' Thames.'

'No wonder you drink shorts', said Steve.

'I serve a good pint here.'

ঋ ঋ ঋ

I knew what Larry was like; I had worked behind the bar with him for a few months. The Queen's is a big pub with two large bars. At the end of each night after all the punters left there was always a lot of clearing up to do. Larry would clear one of the big tables in the bar and we'd collect all the mixers like bitter lemons, tonics, grapefruits, ginger ales, and tomato juices – anything which still had some contents in them. Larry would sit behind the table like Lord Muck smoking one of his iffy King Edward cigars and start bottling and making full ones up. He would then put the metal caps on and put them back on the shelves.

When serving customers who wanted a Teacher's or a Bell's scotch we'd have to walk round to the other bar and put a house scotch in the glass. The punter wouldn't suss it out and Larry was coining it in. If the mild was a bit iffy he'd whack some Guinness in the barrel to liven it up.

He was a tight old git to the staff, so when he was on holiday we'd get our own back. Every year he went out to this apartment in Spain for his two weeks' holiday. But before I tell the story I must tell you about the apartment.

His wife, Olive, was a straight lady and didn't like any villainy. The first time they went there Larry took a mate with them and while they were sunning themselves his mate fitted a burglar alarm and carried out other security jobs in the flat. She thought it was a bit strange and wasn't happy about this bloke being around. The second time they were there, a heavy-duty geezer turned up and parked himself in the spare bedroom. She smelt a rat and had a go at Larry. The long and short of it all was that this flat was a safe house for a couple of London villains, so when somebody was on their toes they came there to lay low. Olive went mad and refused to go there again. She later changed her mind when they both got life sentences and Larry bought the flat from them. That's what Olive thinks; in fact more villains go there to hide than there are in Chelmsford prison.

Anyway back to the pub; while he was away on holiday Larry got one of his cousins, Keith, to run the pub. It was unusual that this family member was a bit divvy. We told Keith, who knew nothing about pubs, that after the boozer closed each night Larry would always give the staff a drink. Larry had these cases of Moët champagne tucked away for very special occasions – so special it got a mention on Police Five. One night we took a lot of money behind the bar and we told Keith that it would be nice to celebrate with some champagne. We pointed him in the direction of the cellar where the champagne was hiding. We drank two cases over the next two nights. When Larry came back he went ballistic and tore into poor old Keith. It was certainly nice to get one over him.

෨ ෨ ෨

After Larry went to check his water bill, his wife Olive came over to Steve and me and had a G&T with us. She mentioned in passing that a girl had come into the pub looking for me a few days back.

'What's she look like,' I asked.

'Oh she was really nice, a very pretty girl.'

Being cocky I said:

'I only go out with good lookers.'

As I was taking a mouthful of beer she said:

'Pity about her long pointed nose and the bump in her tummy, her dad didn't look too happy either.'

The beer flew out of my mouth and nose at a rate of knots, I nearly choked myself.

'She did look a bit worried, Nick; I suppose being pregnant didn't help. I told them you'd be up here this week sometime.'

You know when the blood drains from your face when you hear bad news; I was having one of those moments. Her name was Eve and she came from Grays, and I certainly didn't want to be her Adam. I went out with her for a short time – except for the Ollie Beak she was a fair sort. Suddenly this bloke who looked like he'd just come from the Mr. Universe contest came into the pub, went over to the bar and had a word with Larry. Olive then shouted out loud:

'Oh no, that's the girl's dad.'

Before I could run he came bounding over to me and pulled me up by my collar.

'You're the little toe rag who's got my Eve pregnant.'

'Not me, Guv. Honest.'

'I don't believe yer, you're squirming like a cornered rat.'

I was just about to crap myself when the pub erupted with laughter and my so-called best mate Steve said, with a massive grin on his face:

'I've waited three years to get my own back on you and it was a beauty.'

I have to say he'd done me up like a kipper. He was, of course, referring to the time when I said his girlfriend at the time, Vicky, had a bad dose of pyorrhoea, as I didn't fancy her mate. Of course it was a lie and he'd never forgotten it.

I'd still got a cob on when a bit of light relief came into the pub in the shape of Des (Pot) Smith; he was about the same age as us. He did like a smoke and his greenhouse wasn't cultivating tomatoes! He and his old man had a dodgy car repair business underneath one of the arches at Romford station. Des was a scruffy git, like a walking scarecrow with feet at ten to two, a long neck and even longer nose; he looked like Pinocchio. The motors he bought were usually wrecks and so were his birds, but on this occasion it looked like he'd got himself a nice runner, she seemed a right little darling. He came over to us with his girl.

'Get the beers in,' said Steve to Des.

'Piss off, you're the pop star, you get them in.'

While Steve got the drinks I said to Des:

'Introduce us to your new lady, then.'

'She's off limits to you randy pair, her name is Sara and that's all you need to know.'

Sara took her black Maxi coat off; underneath it she had on a patterned miniskirt, a very tight polo-necked jumper which showed off a fair pair of knockers, and I could smell Arpège perfume. Steve and I had a thing about knowing all the girls' perfumes. I couldn't believe Des had pulled a quality bird, there had to be a catch. Steve bought the drinks back and we all started chatting except Sara, who went to the bog.

'Des, don't think I'm being rude mate, but she's not the norm for you, you normally get them straight from Battersea.'

'That's a bit strong, Steve, are you saying the birds I go out with are dogs?'

'Well, yeah.'

'This one's a little bit tasty; I'm going to have to ask her what she sees in you, Des.'

'Don't you dare, Steve?'

'Des, we're yer mates.'

'Some mates. Look, she brought her motor in the other day for an MOT ...'

'That reminds me, how did you and your old man get on in court last week?' inquired Steve.

'Got a heavy fine and a bit of suspended.'

'How'd you explain to the judge that you'd issued more passed MOTs in a year than any other garage in England? What I read in the newspaper is that it worked out that you would've had to issue a passed MOT every half hour for a whole year including Sundays.'

'Admin error, that's all it was, simple as that, Steve.'

When he said that we burst out laughing. The trouble was he was serious.

'Sara's coming back from the bog, it's now or never, Des.'

'You bastard, Steve. I told her my Aunt May had won the football pools and she's going to give me a nice bundle out of it.'

'Leave it out, Des, she's desolate, I saw her selling pegs in Romford Market last week.'

She came back and sat down at the table. I couldn't help myself.

'Sara, have you ever met Des's Aunty May, she does a nice peg on a Wednesday down the market and ...'

5

First Stop Great Yarmouth

On the morning of the tour, it's the usual aggravations in the Sheldon household. Dad wakes up with the arse ache, all down to vast amounts of Double Diamond consumed the night before with his mates down the Legion. He can't get his Royal Enfield motorbike to start so he gives it a kick, and then has to limp down to the bus stop to get to the brewery where he works. Brother Arthur is looking for a job. I can't see him getting another job as a chef. He's still in bed feeling sorry for himself for being sacked from the hotel after everybody went down with food poisoning. His cranky girlfriend Deirdre turns up looking like bleedin' Che Guevara with this stupid black beret she's got on. She's here to run him to the Labour Exchange. I give her a wink and ask if she fancies a quick one, so she rushes upstairs to Arthur crying that I'm a lecher and for him to sort me out, some chance. Mum is mum and she quietly keeps order as it all kicks off around her.

Steve turns up and we're ready to rock 'n' roll to the first gig at the Regal in Great Yarmouth tonight. There's been a lot of interest, so much so we're booked to play there for two nights. I give my mum a cuddle and a kiss and she warns me to behave and to make sure I keep in contact.

Rick and Tony arrive in the Ford Transit with all the gear loaded in it. The radio is blaring out The Move's 'Night of Fear'. The name of our band is plastered all over the van. It does look the business as we jump in for the trip to Norfolk. Our vinyl is creeping up the charts, so we're well happy.

Steve gets in the driving seat as Rick's a crap driver, and we're off. Looking in the back of the van there's a bleedin' great mattress and what looks like a coffin.

'You expecting company, Rick?'

'I hope so, Nick; I'm fed up having a rumble on a cold metal floor so I thought I'd get a nice soft mattress. Wait till mum and dad get in bed tonight, they won't be happy!'

We all had a giggle.

'What's this coffin doing in between the amps?' I enquire.

'That's my new drum box, Nick, I can store all my hardware in it.'

'Christ, Tone, it's a bit over the top for a few drum sticks.'

Suddenly Steve stops the van and winds down the window. Des, our mate, looking like a bag of shit, is walking up the road.

'Off to Battersea then, Des.'

'Feck' off, Steve.'

We're laughing our heads off as Steve puts the van into first gear. We get to the top of our road, do a left and arrive at our local shops. Our laughter stops immediately. In front of us an old lady is laying in the middle of the road at the Parkfield shops; it appears she's been hit by a car. Her white hair is covered in blood and there's more blood pumping out of her mouth. Dr. Roberts who has a surgery over the road is working on her. We, of course, stop the van and get out offering any help. I recognise her as Des's Aunty May who lives a few doors away from him. Des is close to her as she brought him up when his mum died and his dad went to prison. Dr. Roberts gets up, shakes his head, and takes a blanket from a member of the surgery and covers her with it as the ambulance and police arrive. I look around and I can see Des walking towards the shops. As he arrives I take him to one side:

'Des I'm sorry, mate, I don't know how to say it, that's your Aunt May under the blanket.'

'More piss taking, I suppose.'

'I wish it was. I'm really sorry, Des.'

'Please tell me this is a wind-up, Nick.'

I put my hand on his shoulder as he looks over to the blanket. He rushes over and pushes everybody away and pulls the blanket back. I shall never forget the scream and sobbing as he leant over her.

The police move us on; we don't know whether to stay. Even though we rib him we're good mates. He lives down our street and went to the same school as us. A policewoman takes Des to one side and tries to comfort him. We're really upset for him and feel rotten about pulling his leg minutes before. It's the first dead body any of us have seen.

We decide to leave as his family will take care of him. There's no music on and nothing is said for an hour as we head down the A12, lost in our thoughts.

❧ ❧ ❧

Life came back to normal when Tony farted and we all had to bale out of the van. The weather was quite warm for a winter's day as we arrived at the Regal about mid afternoon, a large old Victorian building with a fair-sized dance floor. The manager let us in and we set up on stage. There were no roadies to help so it was all hands to the pumps. After a quick sound check we went to find our digs. As we were here for two nights we hoped they'd be half decent. They were crap, somebody was having a laugh. We were booked into a hostel for down and outs. It was grim and we asked Rick what his dad was up to. He shrugged his shoulders and said nothing.

We were now at the business end as we checked everything on the stage. It all looked good as the hall filled up. The management had brought some sandwiches in for us and we had a few beers.

We were ready to go and went on stage to a great reception from the packed hall. Tonight was all our own material and just a few covers. We went straight into 'Suburban Mod' and that proved the right move as everybody was partying.

I always laugh at the girls when they first get on the dance floor. They put their handbags on the floor and dance around them until they get pulled by a bloke.

The sweat was pouring off us and the riffs were fast and furious. The first set went well and we opened the second set with 'Hang On Sloopy' by The McCoys. There was a bit of agg' as a couple of likely lads decided to jump off the balcony into the arms of their mates. The bouncers appeared like the cavalry and threw them out.

We'd played the best in ages and it was a top night. We didn't have to load the gear into the van as we were playing there again the next night. Rick seemed to have a bird in every town in England and he disappeared like a ferret down a hole. Mentioning ferrets reminds me of a bloke we knew called Toby, nicknamed 'Ferret Face'. He'd a load of them and he took them hunting. We saw him in Hornchurch one day and he offered Steve and me a lift home. Well, when we got in the Morris Minor the ferrets had eaten their way through the upholstery. It was like travelling in a stock car but he didn't seem to notice or care.

Back to our night's entertainment, Tony prefers to be the lone ranger when looking for girls so he went his own way. Steve and I decided to go to a local coffee bar, Acropolis, for a wind down.

It had been a long day and with the sadness of the accident and the gig, it was just nice to chill out. The bar was packed out as a lot of people had gone to our gig. They were coming over to us saying how much they'd enjoyed it, so much so that a lot of them were coming back the next night to see us again. We were having frothy coffees and listening to 'Sunshine Superman' by Donovan on the jukebox when Steve looked at me and nodded towards two girls who were sitting near us. They were both ten out of ten and as luck would have it the two people sitting opposite at the red Formica table got up to leave. We were over there in two seconds flat giving it the big one.

'Can we join you,' I said.

'Looks like you have,' said one of them in a rich Norfolk accent.

'Some more coffee, girls?'

'Why not,' said the same girl.

'Steve, get the coffees in.'

'What did your last servant die of, Nick?'

Steve left the table and went to get the refills after he sponged half a crown off me. I started speaking to the girl who did the talking, she was called Kay. She had an impish grin and lovely big blue eyes. She'll do for me, I thought. Her mate's name was Val. They were 18 and both had short Twiggy hairstyles. For country girls they dressed well Mod. In fact Val's top was near bursting point. I said to the girls in a bad Norfolk accent:

'It isn't just the turkeys that are 'bootiful' in Norfolk.'

'Is that meant to be some type of compliment,' remarked Kay.

'Well do we look like turkeys then?' said a grinning Val.

You know there's an answer to that, which is a bit naughty, how I stopped myself saying it I don't know. Fortunately

Steve turned up with the coffees though most of it was in the saucers.

'The divvy's been done then,' as he saw me sitting next to Kay.

'You're two of the band members we've just seen at the Regal,' said Kay.

'That's us,' said Steve, 'Hope you enjoyed it.'

'Without it going to your heads we both thought that you're the best band we've seen down here,' said an enthusiastic Kay.

After that it was a match made in heaven. We all got on really well and had a great laugh. When it was chucking out time, we walked them home. It sounds a bit naff when you say you held hands, but hopefully that is the start of things to come. It wasn't going to be tonight, though, as Steve and I were knackered, and anyway there was nowhere to go as they both lived with their parents. We'd a nice snog and then made our way back to the doss house where we were staying. We arranged to see the girls outside the pier the next day. Somehow we navigated back to our digs and saw the Transit outside. When we got up to the van it was rocking, and giggling was coming from inside. Both Steve and I laughed and knocked hard on the back door a couple of times. There was a shuffle and the door opened. A dishevelled Rick stuck his head out.

'What do you two want?'

'We just wondered if you were all right in there, mate, as we heard these funny noises, can we be of any help?'

'I can manage this little jobbee on my own, Nick, now feck off.'

He slammed the door and we burst out laughing again. We rocked the van a few more times, then went into our doss house.

Tony hadn't come back that night so he was up to no good. We'd arranged to be back at the Regal the next day at about five which allowed us a longer sound check before the night's gig.

We met the girls at the pier; the weather was balmy for February with bright sunshine. Steve disappeared with Val, and Kay and I had a walk along the sands. We'd hit it off straightaway and we're enjoying each other's company and having a great laugh. She worked for the local council as a punch card operator. She was bored with Great Yarmouth and her job and wanted to move to London to seek some excitement. As we passed some beach huts I couldn't believe my eyes – coming out of one of them was Tony, looking like death warmed up. Behind him was a bird who certainly wasn't one of Norfolk's beauties. They both looked grim; they must have been hammering away all night to look like that. I said to Kay, taking the piss:

'Have you met our drummer, Tony?'

He was oblivious to it all as he blinked in the sunlight and screwed his eyes up.

'Where am I, Nick?'

'Blackpool.'

'So you're telling me we've done half the tour already then?'

'Tony, just be at the sound check at five and don't be late. And I would suggest a bar of Sunlight soap wouldn't go amiss, as you really pen and ink.'

We were both laughing as we made our way further up the beach. We stopped for a coffee and a donut at a kiosk. We'd a lot in common and had the same sense of humour especially when she said that the girl with Tony was called Alice, nicknamed 'Slack Alice'. She was the local bike, and no band member was safe when they came to Great Yarmouth.

We continued our walk and went past some sand dunes. Sticking up from one of these was a bare hairy arse and it was moving up and down at a fast rate of knots. That arse looked familiar, so we tip-toed nearer and I knew it – it was Steve grunting and groaning and giving it some welly. Kay and I creased up and had to move away. I couldn't believe it, it was only yards from a footpath and he was going like a pneumatic drill. Kay then said, laughing:

'Are you thinking what I'm thinking.'

With that we went hunting for some form of container. We found a couple of empty carrier bags in a nearby bin. We quickly filled them up from the water's edge, hid behind another sand dune and lobbed both bags in their direction. We knew they had hit the mark when Steve shouted out:

'I'm bleedin' soaking here?'

'So am I, is the tide coming in?' said an alarmed Val.

How Kay and I kept it together I don't know. While they quickly got dressed we crept away. I thought it was all very well me laughing but the other three had scored and I was still on a duck. Then, after a bite to eat, I heard those magic words:

'Do you want to come round my house to listen to some music, Nick?'

It was an instant 'I'd love to.' Her parents were out for a couple of hours watching her young brother Clive in a swimming gala.

Kay lived in a small terraced house in St Nicholas Road, which I thought was quite appropriate. They had a yappy mongrel that was locked in the kitchen, luckily. The record player went straight on, a red and white Marconiphone; I had one of those before my Dansette. As 'Sorrow' by The Merseys came on we were on the settee having a good snog. The smell of her Blue Waltz perfume was ramping up the juices. We were all over each other and I could now see her stocking tops, but in the background this mutt was barking for Britain and just wouldn't stop.

'I'm going to have to take it out in the garden and let it do its business, otherwise it's going to wreck the kitchen and my parents will go loopy.'

'Kay, do you have to?'

'I'll be back in a minute Nick, I won't be long.'

She went into the kitchen. I was now on overdrive. I looked at my watch, it was four and our sound check was in an hour, plus her parents could come back at anytime. Kay rushed back in a panic,

'Bobby's escaped.'

'Who's bleedin' Bobby?'

'It's the puppy, mum idolises it. I've got to find it otherwise all hell will let loose.'

'It'll find its own way home, leave it.'

'I can't Nick, it's her baby.'

There I am with a stiffy in my trousers, running up and down her road looking for poxy Bobby. I cornered it up against a wall. As it escaped I tried to give it a kick but it was too quick for me; I kicked the wall instead and did my toe in. We finally caught it and took it home. As Kay opened the front door her parents turned up. Her stupid mum kissed this hound all over. Her dad looked at me and said:

'I think we've come back just in time.'

ৰ ৰ ৰ

Somehow we all got back to the Regal by five. We had a good practice session and then went into the pub opposite. After a few pints of Abbot bitter and Old Bob light ale, we were out of it, talk about strong. The locals called this drink 'Skull

Attack'. We knew we were pissed when we started playing 'Come Tomorrow' by Manfred Mann and Rick was singing 'Summer In The City' by The Lovin' Spoonful. What a cock-up, somehow we got through the first set.

The second set went well and we had a ball. If I say so myself I was playing well and enjoying every minute of it. It was another full house and we were dancing about on stage giving it the biz. After the gig we all met up with our birds. Tony went back to the beach hut with Slack Alice while Rick took his girl back to his Vono spring mattress in the back of the van. Steve and I and the two girls went back to the coffee bar where we first met as it was pissing down with rain and there was nowhere else to go. Kay and I were holding hands and being a bit lovey dovey. She then whispered in my ear:

'Sorry we didn't get it together, Nick.'

'That's okay, just being with you was just as nice, Kay.'

Steve overheard what we said and opened his mouth like he was being sick. He and Val were really taking the rise. I have to hand it to Kay when she said to the both of them:

'Was it raining on the sand dunes today?'

'So it was you two who chucked the water over us, then,' said Steve as Val went bright red.

The wind-ups went on all night between us. When it was time to go I walked Kay home and we said our goodbyes; she really was a nice girl and in one way I hoped we'd meet again.

The next day we collected Tony from his residence on the beach. It had turned really cold that night and when he came out of the beach hut with Slack Alice he looked like a frozen turd. We picked up our gear from the Regal and were on our way to the next gig in Norwich. We had two phone calls to make so when we stopped for a greasy, we used the phone outside the cafe. I phoned my mum and asked her to send a wreath on behalf of the band for Des's aunt's funeral. Rick made the next call to his dad to see how our record was going. It was now number 28 in the charts, but he didn't reckon it would go much further. That was a disappointment, but when you are up against the likes of The Beatles, Stones, Hollies, and The Who, it wasn't a bad result for your first record.

Oh yeah, Rick's old man added that there was a cash flow problem and there'd be no more accommodation on the first part of the tour. Sleeping in a van in the winter was not my idea of fun. I was having serious doubts about Rick's dad being our manager. Both Steve and Tony had spoken to me about their concerns and we knew we'd have to front Rick up about it soon.

It's not a high-paying job being a musician unless you are in one of the top bands. In the music industry they have a saying for it:

'What's a musician without a girlfriend?'

'Homeless.'

6

Boils & Nurses at Derby

It wasn't a good gig at Norwich, for whatever reason we played crap, however we did have a laugh. Rick's dad had let us down badly on the accommodation front. I wondered if he'd got the hump with his son after he nicked the mattress. It was going to be a night in the van; you can imagine it, four blokes in a Transit. We've all had a good few beers and large portions of savaloys and chips. The piss taking and farting was at a record high and something had to give.

'You lot are bleedin' animals I've had enough of this,' said Tony.

And with that he emptied his drum box, dragged it outside and banged the van doors behind him; he was going to sleep in the coffin tonight. Overnight it had gone from quite mild to brass monkey weather. When we woke up we looked through the windows; there'd been a severe frost. The drum box had gone from brown to white. We jumped out of the van and opened it. Tony was still asleep, wrapped up in his sleeping bag with just his head showing. Looking closer we roared with laughter; his bushy eyebrows were now snow white, they were covered in frost. After prising him out of his box we all went to the public bog for a cold wash, then on to the nearest greasy spoon for a fry up before going to our next gig. After Norwich we did a few more venues in East Anglia then it was off to Peterborough, Nottingham, and on to Derby.

ॐ ॐ ॐ

I hadn't told the other lads but I had this gigantic boil on my bum; I couldn't sit down and was in agony. So when we arrived in Derby I sloped off to the nearest hospital. I was lucky it wasn't busy and they saw me straight away, putting me into a cubicle. I'm not that brave at the best of times so I was crapping myself. In walked this old dragon who looked like the senior nurse, she certainly wasn't Florence Nightingale. She looked at my admission card and with boredom in her voice said:

'So you've a boil on your right buttock, then, Mr. Sheldon.'

'Well, yeah.'

'You'd better get your trousers off, then.'

I dropped me strides and stood there in my Thunderbirds underpants, which didn't impress her.

'And them, please,' she said, pointing to my underpants.

Then she asked me to bend over the bed. I felt a right twat as I bent over.

'That's a big one and it's got a nice head on it,' she remarked.

Being clever I said with a grin:

'You sure it's the boil you're looking at, nurse.'

'Mr. Sheldon, I've seen all sorts, and I'm afraid cheap jokes like that just go straight over my head.'

She disappeared out of the cubicle leaving me lost for words. Within a couple of minutes she was back with a young nurse who looked scared of the old dragon and was listening to every word she uttered.

'Mr. Sheldon has a nasty boil on his right buttock. We'll give him an antibiotic injection, as we don't know what has caused this.'

She produced this bleedin' long needle and had great delight in sticking it in my arse. After the screams subsided she asked the young nurse:

'What can cause these abscesses, Nurse Randall?'

Looking extremely uncomfortable, she replied:

'Usually a hair root caused by a staphylococcus or if the patient keeps having these it could be lowered vitality of the skin. It could also suggest a number of other causes including general health and attention to skin, hygiene and physical exhaustion.'

'I'm very impressed, Nurse Randall, that's very good.'

The old dragon looked at me snidely, and said, with my boil pulsating and me in extreme pain:

'In the case of Mr. Sheldon I would think it is the latter. We'll quickly lance the boil and get him on his way, as we've more deserving patients needing our attention.'

And with that she was out the door. Nurse Randall looked at me and we both burst out laughing.

'She didn't get the pass certificate at the charm school course she attended, then?'

'No, Sister Cotton does have a way with her, especially to us junior nurses.'

'What's your name?'

'Nurse Randall.'

'Bleedin' hell, are you all like this in Derby?'

'Sorry, it's Helen. Right we need to get this boil lanced.'

While she was working on my boil I had a good look at her. She was about my age, quite plain, a bit mumsy but nice. I could tell she had stockings on as there was a ridge on both legs halfway up her skirt. She looked up and said:

'What are you doing in Derby then?'

'I'm playing a gig tonight at the Surf dance hall.'

The excitement on her face when I said that was making her forget why I was here.

'You're part of Modern Edge, then?' she said all excitedly.

'Well yeah, I'm the lead guitarist.'

'I bought your record last week and I'm going with my best friend Lesley to your gig. All the nurses who are not on duty are coming, and then we're going to a party at one of their houses afterwards, its Sally's 19th birthday.'

As soon as she said party my ears were like Jodrell Bank. Then those immortal words:

'I'm sure Sally would love you to come, I mean you lot are famous.'

I was feeling a bit big-headed, and then Helen struck gold and pus shot out everywhere; my screams echoed around the hospital again.

'Sorry about that, Nick. It should feel a lot better now.'

'I can see why men don't have babies – that really hurt.'

'You can get dressed now, it's all over.'

I quickly put my clothes back on as I was feeling a bit self-conscious about having no pants on. It didn't seem to bother her. I knew I was feeling better when there was a bit of movement down below. She looked at me and grinned:

'I seem to have made an impression, then?'

I went as red as a beetroot. Although embarrassed I still made arrangements to see her after the gig.

కు కు కు

The Surf certainly wasn't one of the finest places we'd played at, but it was the biggest. From the outside it looked like a prison. Next door was a swimming pool which was brilliant. We enjoyed a swim and a welcome shower. The hall might have been a dump but the people inside it were really nice and they gave us some great home-made food, courtesy of the manager's wife Phyllis. The stage was enormous. They reckoned there could be a good few hundred people there that night. That made us all really nervous so we made sure the sound check was spot on.

I'd told the others there might be a party after the gig, so it could be a good night all round. Once we'd set up, Rick wanted to have a word with us, so we went back to the dressing room. It was Steve's turn to flash the ash and he got out a packet of Weights which looked like they'd been in his pocket for a while as they were all squashed. We lit up and swigged from some bottles of brown ale. Rick was worried about the lack of sleeping arrangements on the tour. He was also concerned that not all the expenses were filtering through to us. He'd gone to the bank and there was only half the amount that there should've been. He'd phoned his dad but couldn't get a straight answer from him. Rick was one of our own and he was clearly embarrassed about his father. We couldn't do anything about it until the second part of the tour when we had a couple of days off. But we were pleased he'd brought the subject up and it had now cleared the air between us.

There was an edge in the room as Phyllis came in and said the hall was full, which gave us a real buzz. We were wearing our new baggy jeans, regency collar shirts and black winkle pickers with zips up the side, and were ready to play. What a night, it was the best we'd played in a long time. The revellers were well up for it and appeared to enjoy it as much as we did. At the end of the two hours, we played an extra half an hour which went down well. Afterwards Steve, Tony and I went to the nurse's party while Rick did his own thing. We agreed to meet back at the van at 10 o'clock the following morning. We had a free day before our next gig in Manchester, so we were all hoping to bed down somewhere, hopefully not on our own.

&v &v &v

Helen had gone from looking a bit mumsy to a raving beauty, what a transformation. She'd scrubbed up so well, I was now in love. Lesley had paired up with Tony while Steve was with another one of the nurses called Marilyn, She didn't look like Monroe, but she was a fair bint.

It was quite an intimate party of about 30 people. There was only one bedroom so it was plenty of dancing and booze. While dancing close with Helen to Jimmy Ruffin's 'What Becomes Of The Broken Hearted', her perfume of Blue Waltz was drifting up and giving me the urge, so it was now time to try and see what was going to happen after the party.

'It's going to be a bit cold sleeping in the van tonight, Helen.'

There was no answer so I threw another one in:

'Especially on a cold van floor in the depth of winter.'

Nothing, not a murmur from her. When the record stopped she went over to a pile of 45s that was lying on the floor. She when slowly through them, much to the annoyance of the other dancers, including Steve who shouted:

'I didn't know your bird was a DJ, she could get a job on Radio London.'

I shouted back to Steve and said:

'Do you know we were just talking about you?'

'Something nice I hope.'

'Yeah, Helen reckons you played bass guitar tonight like you had a pair of boxing gloves on.'

'Bollocks.'

After what seemed ages she put a record on the turntable. She came back over to me smiling as the Rolling Stones 'Let's Spend The Night Together' came on. After that it was all systems go as we went into the hallway for a quick snog. We were all over each other and I said with a grin:

'My place or yours?'

'I'm not going back to your dirty old van, and who says we're spending the night together. You can't come back to the nurses' home, visitors are strictly forbidden, especially boys.'

'But the record,' I said.

'Nick, never assume that what you hear is what you get.'

About an hour later I walked her home, which was about a mile away. It was just starting to snow as we arrived back at the nurse's home. I kissed her goodnight and started to make my way back to the van although I had no idea where it was. Then there was a call from heaven:

'Would you like a coffee?'

I turned around towards Helen so quickly I felt dizzy. I laughed and said:

'Only if it's a cup of Camp!'

'Just one thing, Nick, they've got a security bloke patrolling the nurses' quarters so you've got to be really quiet. He's a creep. Go around to the back and I will let you in through the fire escape door, but be quiet.'

She opened the door quickly and within a minute or so I was in her room on the second floor. As it happens we did have a quick coffee and then nature took its course. Halfway through the night we heard a shuffle outside in the courtyard. Then it went quiet and then a scraping noise and then a thump as something appeared to be put up against the wall. Then it all went quiet again. We're just about to have seconds when there was a loud shout, then a scream, which sounded familiar.

'Help, help, I need some help here quickly, I'm going to fall.'

We jumped out of bed and looked out of the window; the snow was still falling. As I looked out I couldn't believe my eyes. There was Tony looking like Father Christmas, hanging on for dear life to a ladder which had slipped as he was trying to get into Lesley's room. Windows opened from all directions to find out what all the racket was about. One of them was Steve who was above me on the third floor. He shouted down to me:

'What's he doing up a ladder, he gets giddy if the stage he's playing on is a bit high? The dickhead, I'm just about to sample the fruits of Derby and I've got to go and save his skin.'

Both Steve and I rushed down with a couple of other blokes who were staying overnight at the nurses' home. The security geezer also turned up, not happy that he hadn't caught any of us creeping in. While we were trying to get Tony down he was going on about us breaking and entering the nurses' home and that he was going to call the police, which he did. We finally got the idiot down from the ladder and the three of us ran off to the sound of sirens and bells from the police and the fire brigade. The snow was now coming down in bucket loads and the three of us were freezing our nuts off. We hadn't got a clue where we were. By luck we found an all-night cafe near the market area, ordered mugs of tea and egg sarnies and tried to dry ourselves off.

'Tony, why was you up a ladder when you can't stand heights?' asked a bemused Steve.

'If you were on a promise, wouldn't you do it?'

'I was on a promise till you cocked it all up.'

'By the way, where did you get that ladder from?' I asked.

'Well the fire escape had been locked. Then Lesley the bird I was with told me about the caretaker's shed. I broke into it and nicked the ladder.'

This arab-looking bloke brought us the egg sandwiches which we gobbled down in record time. As I was eating I was looking around the dingy cafe. I saw this small stuffed camel on a shelf which reminded me of a funny story my Uncle Cyril told me about.

ᗌ ᗌ ᗌ

Cyril fought in the desert in the war and a while back they'd organised a reunion of his army mates in Egypt or somewhere like that. Everywhere you went they had these stuffed camels on sale. They went on a trip on a small ferry with loads of other people. Near enough everyone had bought one of these camels to take home with them. It was a bit choppy and wet so all the passengers went into the lounge. After a while there was this really terrible smell and everyone was heaving, including the staff who complained to the captain. The captain slowed the ferry down in the middle of the sea and said he wasn't going any further until all the camels were thrown overboard. Of course the question had to be asked why? The reason was that these camels were stuffed with camel shit. Because it was so wet and damp the shit was emulsifying and giving off this horrendous stink. Cyril was used to smells as he worked down Billingsgate fish market in London, but even he said that this was something else. As the ferry moved off all you could see were loads of camels floating in the sea.

ᗌ ᗌ ᗌ

We left the cafe about eight; the cafe owner was as good as gold and had allowed us to stay even though we didn't buy any more food and drinks. It had stopped snowing and he pointed us in the right direction, back to the Surf about three miles away. We left him closely examining his stuffed camel, making sure it wasn't stuffed with camel shit.

♪ 7 ♪

On the Road to Manchester

It took us half an hour to clear the snow and ice off the van. Rick hadn't shown up yet but we had said we'd be back at the van by 10.00 for our journey to Manchester. We wanted to make sure there weren't any cock-ups as this was going to be the biggest venue we'd be playing on the first part of the tour. On opening the van we found a piece of paper stuck on the steering wheel from Rick. It simply said,

'See you at the The Royal, Manchester tomorrow.'

Rick had never let us down so we took it as read that he'd be there. Knowing Rick he'd pulled a bird with a motor and she was going to take him to the gig.

After Phyllis opened up we put our gear in the van. Without Rick we had no money for diesel as he was looking after all the travelling expenses, so we had to walk to the local Post Office and drain our accounts out, which we were not too happy about.

Back in the van Tony turned the key in the ignition, nothing; the battery was as dead as a dodo. If this was being a pop star I'd go back to selling motors. We'd got hardly any money, our clothes were stinking and Rick's dad was ripping us off. We were living in a van and eating shit food, but playing to big audiences and we'd got a record in the top thirty – something was wrong somewhere.

None of us were very good with motors so we were sitting there like spare pricks at a wedding. Tony handed out the Kensitas tipped and we were looking for divine intervention.

With no sleep for over twenty four hours this didn't help our tempers. Phyllis came out of the hall and we told her our problem. Our saviour was on the plot straight away. She called the local garage and about an hour later a young lad our age turned up; he looked a bit naive. He couldn't jump start it, he said the battery was dead and we'd need a new one. No chance, we were potless. He was quite impressed that he was helping a band he'd seen play the night before so I worked on that.

'What's your name?'

'Sammy.'

'Sammy, you've probably got some more motors to call on that won't start because of the cold weather.'

'Yeah, I've got another four calls.'

'How'd you like a signed copy of our latest record?'

'Ace, that'd be tasty, my bird would love that.'

'It's yours, Sammy; it's all right to call you Sammy, I'm Nick.'

'Of course, Nick.'

'I need a little favour in return, mate. I'm sure when you call on these four motors one of them will only need a jump start.'

'Most of the time that's all it is,' replied Sammy, looking important.

'What I need you to do Sammy is to tell one of them that their battery is worn out. They buy a new one from you and you can fit their one into our van.'

It all went quiet until Steve said:

'Sammy, when we're up here again, which should be soon, we'll give you two free tickets for you and your bird and you can be our guests. How's that grab yer?'

'I don't know about that, that's lying to customers.'

'Just think about it,' said Steve in his poor me voice. 'You're helping us out big time and your boss will be as happy as Larry, you've got him an order for a nice new battery.'

It went so quiet I thought somebody had bleedin' died. In sales this is what's called a golden silence close. You ask for the order and wait for the punter's answer, in this case Sammy.

'Are you going to do a dodgy battery for us?'

Once you've asked the question, you don't say another word until they open their mouth. So all three of us said nothing and looked Sammy straight in the eye. He was looking very apprehensive, opened his mouth and coughed. That was our in. We were all over him like a rash saying thanks for doing that for us, mate. Sammy was overwhelmed with the attention and agreed to do it.

While he was away Phyllis allowed us to stay in the foyer. We all lay down on the seats and had a kip. A couple of hours later Sammy did the business and fitted a half decent battery in the van. We also got him to check the van over for water, oil and tyre pressures. He had his signed record and was happy. We always carry a few boxes of signed copies around with us to impress the birds.

We made our way slowly to Manchester; what a poxy journey. There was snow everywhere and the landscape was a total white-out. If we'd been playing that night we wouldn't have got there in time. Tony was driving as we put the eight-track stereo on. Steve and I gave it the air guitar as The Who's 'My Generation' came on and Tony was doing his drum beat on the steering wheel. What a great record – we played it over and over again. Then the fun stopped, the needle on the fuel indicator was at zero, we were running out of diesel in the middle of nowhere and virtually broke. When we'd raided our Post Office accounts we ended up with about five quid between us. We soldiered on looking for a garage to fill up. There was a signpost for Congleton, so hopefully there'd be a garage there. Tony suddenly veered to the left and went down a short dirt track leading to a farm and came to an abrupt halt.

❧ ❧ ❧

'I've got an idea lads, follow me,' says Tony.

Steve and I get out of the van, not knowing what he's up to and walk up to the farmhouse. This large wooden door looms up in front of us. Tony gets hold of the iron knocker and gives it a wallop, the sound must have echoed around the farm, what a noise it made. There's no answer so Tony gives it another whack. Suddenly the door opens. Standing there is this old boy with a face like a smacked arse.

'I'm sorry to trouble you, sir,' says a polite Tony. 'I'm wondering if you have any red diesel we could buy from you?'

'What've you got then, a feckin' tractor,' says the sarcastic old bastard. 'Get off my property. I don't want long-haired scruffy southern louts like you knocking on my door.'

The door rocks back on its hinges as it slams shut.

'That worked really well, mate, I'm well impressed,' says Steve.

I chip in and say:

'Yeah, if you've any more bright ideas like that, Tone, just keep them to yourself.'

We get back in the van and make our way out of the farm. After about ten yards Tony slams on the anchors.

'Do you see what I see, that looks like a tank over there, I wonder if that's where that old git keeps his diesel?'

Tony quickly manoeuvres the van over to the tank. We're out of the van in seconds. Tony goes over to the tank and tries to turn the tap on which appears to be frozen. Steve gets a hammer out of the van and gives the tap a right clump, still no movement, so he gives it another one, you could've heard the noise in Manchester. Suddenly the tap disintegrates into bits and there's diesel pissing out of the hole where the tap should've been. It's like Custer's last stand as we get the bucket which we keep hanging under the back of the van. We use this when we need an emergency number two. We put the bucket under the hole and then fill up our fuel tank in the van. The smell of diesel is rife. Within a few minutes there are shouts coming from all over the farm. We dive back in the van, Tony puts it in first and we're away, unfortunately not where we want to go. The van slips on the ice and we demolish a five-bar wooden gate and end up in a field.

It's pandemonium as Tony drives across the field. Steve and I are shouting at him to slow down. He heads for another gate at the end of the field. Steve jumps out and tries to push it open, but it's got a padlock on it. The trusty hammer comes out again and he starts knocking the crap out of it. In the distance coming towards us is a Land Rover with its headlights on and a tractor. Steve gets back in the van in a panic:

'The bleedin' thing won't move.'

'Hang on,' says Tony.

With that Tony reverses the van, revs it up and with full throttle goes forward and drives straight through it and demolishes another wooden gate. We hit the road and he's driving like Graham Hill as we fly down the country lanes. The snow has eased off but the road conditions are still treacherous. We finally get back on the main road and stop at the next transport cafe. We hide the van behind it so that it can't be seen from the road. We jump out and spend our last couple of bob on a giant fry-up. While we're there a couple of police cars roar by with lights flashing, the full works. Whether they were after us we didn't know.

ॐ ॐ ॐ

It was now 9.00 and we'd made the food last as long as possible as we weren't looking forward to sleeping in a frozen van smelling of red diesel. Steve then said with a laugh:

'Yeah, if the police find us in there we'll be caught red-handed!'

While we're there a Bedford van came into the car park at speed and slid to a stop. On the side of the van was the name of a band, called 'Bad Brakes', no wonder. As they entered the cafe they were just like us, noisy bastards. They were taking the piss out of one of their group members who was having a bad hair day. We later found out that he'd fallen asleep in the van and they'd cut nearly all his hair off, he wasn't a happy bunny. We introduced ourselves and hit it off immediately. They were a four-piece from Barnet in North London and were on their way to Warrington to play a gig. They were a bit younger than us and were great lads. I took to the singer Ray straight away; we both had the same taste in music and humour. The other three members of the band were Eric who played rhythm guitar, Denny minus his hair on bass, and Billy on drums. As we were skint they bought us some more teas. With a laugh I asked Ray:

'How'd you come up with the name Bad Brakes?'

'We were called 'The Feds', then somebody said there was already a band by that name. We seemed to go through gig vans like there's no tomorrow. They were all heaps of shit and Carl our previous drummer would moan that they all had bad brakes. In fact Carl was spot on, the brakes gave up on our last van and we hit a lorry-load of sheep down in Suffolk, what a mess that was. There were more sheep in the road than there are in Wales. After that Carl jacked the band in. So we called ourselves Bad Brakes for a laugh. The only problem with the name is that we keep getting stopped by the Old Bill checking our brakes!'

'Yeah, in fact,' said Billy, 'we've just had a tug by the law. Someone with a van has just nicked a load of diesel from a farm; we're in the clear, we run on petrol.'

'That's a pity,' said a grinning Steve, 'We've got a bit of spare capacity to sell!'

'You lot nicked the diesel then,' said Eric. 'Good luck to yer; we're always siphoning petrol on tour. We should've called the band the BP Boys.'

The wind-ups lasted into the early morning. We had a lot of things in common with them as we played a lot of the same numbers. They'd had a few acetates made of songs they wrote which they were trying to plug with record companies. Acetate is a record cut from a master tape. It looks like a 45rpm. The only problem with it, it's made from Shellac which is a very soft substrate. Because it's soft you can only play it a few times before it deteriorates.

Their management sounded like Rick's dad, a bunch of crooks. They'd got them travelling around the country working for peanuts. In fact the gig in Warrington was for one of the directors who owned a string of record shops. He was opening a new shop there and wanted a London band to provide the music at the opening. They were then on a short tour of the North-west and then back down to London.

The gig at the shop was in the afternoon so we invited them to our show in Manchester, which they said they'd definitely come along to. We'd some beers in the van and shared them with the Barnet lads.

Both bands slept in their vans in the car park overnight. We felt guilty in the morning when they bought us breakfast. We said that when they came to the gig tonight the beers would be on us.

8

Trouble in Manchester

Our record actually got to 25 in the charts. We were disappointed that it hadn't got any further but we were working on other material which hopefully would take us further up the charts next time.

Rick's dad was never contactable while we were on tour; it looked like he'd disappeared off the face of the earth. We spoke to Anthony our agent, sometimes known as the booker, who seemed pretty straight. He'd got some great gigs for us which should've paid well. The problem was that all the money we earnt went to Rick's dad. As our manager he would divvy it up for the band, same with the record company's money. It was worrying as we were working hard and not getting what we were due.

That night's venue was as big as it got for us. The Royal was one of the biggest halls in Manchester so we were looking forward to playing there. We couldn't get into it till about 4.00 so we were at a loose end. Matt Busby's Manchester United, with the likes of Denis Law, Bobby Charlton and George Best, were playing at home. We could have at least seen the first half but with no money it was hopeless. The money situation was now so bad we even thought about jacking the tour in. We couldn't even ruck Rick because he wasn't here. We'd just finished the last packet of five Dominos, which is like smoking a mixture of leaves and grass. Then an excited Tony said:

'The lads from Barnet have given me a great idea. Steve, drive to the main shopping centre.'

Steve just shrugged his shoulders and looked at me as if to say 'another great idea'. Steve followed the signs for the shopping centre and stopped in Market Street. While Steve stayed with the van I followed Tony who was on a mission. We stopped at a large record shop and went inside. Tony asked for the manager. This guy was in his late twenties, a ringer for John Lennon with his round rimless glasses and military jacket, came over to us. The guy introduced himself as Sean Nolan and he had a strong Irish accent. I had to give it to Tony, he really came up with the dog's bollocks of an idea for us to get some instant readies, and enjoy it at the same time.

Sean was up for the craic and Tony suggested that we'd come into the shop now and play a few numbers including 'Suburban Mod'. We'd use our records in the van, which cost us nothing, to sell to the punters. He'd get his normal buying price rate but wouldn't have to pay for them so it was all bunce money for him. Of course we'd pocket the rest which should be a nice few bob. As a lever for them to buy the record they'd all be signed on the cover by us.

Within the hour we'd set up and were ready to play. With no Rick I had to sing as Steve is tone deaf and Tony's got a voice like a croaking frog. Talk about a result. By early afternoon we'd sold the lot. Sean was happy as a dog with two dicks. We left there with a nice wedge in our pockets and headed for the nearest Wimpy. On the way we stopped at Tesco's and pushed the boat out buying three packs of 20 Senior Service; normally sold at 5/5d a pack, they were on special offer at five bob a pack.

Most of the places we played at, the people who ran them were great, but not this time. As soon as we clapped eyes on the promoter of this gig, there was an instant dislike. You could see he didn't like people from south of Watford. He was about 40 and dressed like a teenager. He had a large cigar on and wore these red tinted glasses. He thought he was the King of Manchester pop. He was name dropping every band you've ever heard of like they were his mates. We were shown into the dressing room which was a khazi. It was even worse than our van. While we were setting up he came over and said:

'The last band that played here didn't get paid because they were crap, so be warned, and don't have any ideas of using the PA system here; the last lot blew it up.'

Steve went up to him and eyeballing him, said:

'We always get paid, so don't start mugging us off.'

He didn't like that and came back with:

'I've paid for a four-piece band I see there's only three of you, that will break the contract in my eyes, so in three hours time there'd better be four of you.'

After throwing that in, he walked away with a smug grin. All three of us had been worrying about Rick's no-show; it was now turning into a major problem. I went out and phoned his house, there was no reply. I rang the agent. In fact I think I rang everybody who knew him. I even rang a few hospitals to see whether there'd been any accidents – all drew a blank.

❧ ❧ ❧

There was also a worry, that with the size of the large hall our Vox 30s wouldn't have enough amplification, as one of the amps was on the blink and we had a faulty speaker. We were going to take them into a music shop to see if they could repair them, but with no money that was dead in the water.

We set up the gear on stage and had a sound check. We looked at the vast hall in front of us which would be filled to the gunnels soon. I didn't normally get nervous before a gig but I could see this turning into a disaster. We trooped back into the cold, depressing dressing room, no grub lined up here. The arsehole of a promoter walked in again and said sarcastically:

'Where's the other band member then?'

'He's gone to get a tray of free drinks from your bar manager,' said Tony. 'He knows him really well. If you see him tell him to hurry up as we're dying of thirst.'

He was out of the room in a flash. As he dashed out the door a young guy came in. I said to this bloke:

'Why's your boss such a shit?'

'You're from London way aren't you?'

'Well, yeah.'

'About six months ago a five-piece band from London came here to play. When they left the next day they had six members.'

'I don't get it.'

'His missus ran off with the drummer and hasn't been seen since. So anybody with a southern accent is now public enemy number one. By the way there are four guys at the stage door who're saying you're expecting them. Do you want me to bring them up?'

'Yeah, show them in,' I replied.

The four boys from Bad Brakes bounced in. They'd come straight from their gig in Warrington. They still had their working clothes on which were white Ben Sherman shirts, Levi jeans and blue and white baseball boots. They were well impressed with the venue as they normally only played to a hundred or so people at the most.

Why are most lead singers good looking? Ray had short, blond, nearly whitish hair, bright blue eyes and a smile that must give him the pick of the girls.

We had some bottles of Boddingtons bitter, brewed locally at Strangeways Brewery in Manchester. We handed them out to the boys from Barnet and dished out the Senior Service. We'd two hours to go and there was still no Rick. We now had to go into plan B but none of us had a clue what that was. We explained our problem to Ray and his lads. Ray then couldn't get his words out quick enough as a spray of bitter hit me straight in the face. With a big grin he said:

'It ain't a problem, it's an opportunity. You're now looking at the lead singer of Modern Edge. What do you think then, boys, and Eric could play rhythm for yer?'

It all went quiet for a moment then Steve said excitedly:

'That's a great shout Ray.'

Tony and I had to agree that it would solve most of our problems. Although we didn't know this band and they could be crap, we'd run out of options so it was agreed it was a goer. We had less than two hours to get a couple of sets put together. It would be all covers and I would sing our chart number. We quickly wrote down the songs that we all knew. After a few minutes we came up with a few numbers which included, 'On A Carousel' by The Hollies', 'Paint It Black' by the Stones, 'Substitute' by The Who, and 'Sha La La La Lee', by The Small Faces.

Once we'd got some idea of what we were playing we went straight on stage and rehearsed some of the numbers. They set up a couple of their Marshall amps and speakers alongside ours. Ray's singing suited us fine; he had a good voice and was a live wire on stage. Eric was steady on rhythm and kept it nice and simple. We were still hoping Rick would show but with only ten minutes to go before we were on it seemed unlikely.

≈ ≈ ≈

It was time to start the gig; we all shook hands and wished each other luck. This is the time when the butterflies kick in and you're hoping it all goes well. The walk from the dressing room to the stage was quite a distance. We knew we were near when we could hear the noise from the packed hall. We got a great reception as we picked up our guitars. It was rammed to the rafters and they were all waiting for the first chord to be struck. Ray looked at me, gave the nod and we went straight into 'The House Of The Rising Sun' by The Animals. There was no room to dance so everyone was just bobbing to the music.

Once we got the first number out of the way we were more relaxed and gave it the gun. Ray was in his element, having never sung to so many people before. The atmosphere was electric as we went into the last number and the first set was a winner.

We made our way back to the dressing room and had a few beers. Billy, Denny, Tony and Steve were in a huddle in the corner, probably up to no good. After a short break we were back on for the second set. Ray looked at me as we started with 'Mr. Tambourine Man' by The Byrds. I was so engrossed in getting the chord changes right that I didn't notice what was happening behind me until I saw Steve and Tony with two birds on the dance floor. I turned around quickly and saw Billy on drums and Denny on bass. As it happens they kept the beat well and it was a bit of an edge playing with another band. We had to go straight into 'Keep On Runnin' by The Spencer Davis Group. This had a nice little lick on the bass which Denny played well. As we were finishing the number I could see Steve's face when he heard Denny's great bass playing. He and Tony were back on stage pronto for the next number. When we finished the song I said quickly to Steve:

'I think the band's just found a new bass player.'

'Bollocks, in your dreams.'

The night was a success and playing with new musicians was a great experience and fun. We were all bubbly as we made our way back to the dressing room.

As we entered the room I couldn't believe it, there was scruffy Des looking like Jack-the-lad.

'How yer going boys,' piped up Des, 'You're now looking at your new tour manager.'

Rick was sitting in the corner looking very sheepish.

Des was wearing a long, black, leather jacket with a matching pork pie hat, black jeans and the longest pair of winkle-pickers I'd ever seen. They were so pointed you could burst balloons with them. He had this cannabis plant hanging out of his mouth and he was puffing away like he owned the place. Rick got up slowly from his chair and said:

'I appreciate you're owed an explanation for my no-show and of course you'll get one. As it happens, listening to my stand-in I might not even have a job now. I'll explain everything to you tomorrow morning before we go to the next venue in Bolton. Tonight the drinks are on me and I've organised digs for us tonight, so bear with me and all will be explained.'

Just then the promoter walked in and said sarcastically:

'I thought I was booking Modern Edge not a stand-in band. I don't know whether I'm going to pay you.'

I shouted over to Des and said:

'If you're our tour manager you'd better sort this tosser out so we get our wedge.'

'No problem, Nick, consider it done.'

Des is a wily bastard and can look after himself. He got hold of the promoter and dragged him outside the room to give him his life story and get our money.

❧ ❧ ❧

True to his word Rick splashed the cash for both bands at the club we ended up at. We really wanted to find out why Rick had let us down and why he'd brought Des along, but we held off till the next day. What a party we had that night. We met a bunch of girls as you do and all of us had a great time. Des was in his element and he came up with the joke of the night.

Doreen, one of the girls we were with, wore this ultra miniskirt. This was great, but being about 18 stone, with legs like tree trunks, it wasn't a pretty sight. Des didn't care and he latched on to her, he liked them big, raw and ugly. When he told her he was the tour manager she couldn't leave him alone. It was embarrassing as they were down each other's throats all night. When they eventually came up for air, and after about six pints, Des stood up and said to everybody:

'You've got to hear this joke it's a real laugh – if miniskirts get any shorter, said the frog to the spider, there'll be two more cheeks to powder and much more hair to comb.'

We all creased up with laughter.

After a great night we went back to the digs Rick had organised. As the boys from Bad Brakes had nowhere to sleep except for their van we doubled up with them in our rooms. That was the least we could do for them after all the help they'd given us.

The next morning we said goodbye to Ray and his boys and agreed to keep in touch with each other.

9

Dodgy Management but the Show Goes On

Well before breakfast Des was dispatched to have a look at the van. There was some damage on it after demolishing two five-bar gates. This included two smashed headlights, a front bumper hanging off and a leaking radiator. He was a wizard with motors and hopefully could do something with it.

Over a late breakfast Rick told us about his disappearing act. He explained to us that he was well pissed off with his father in the way he was treating the band, the lack of accommodation on the tour and the shortfall of expenses. He was also concerned that money due to us from the record company and our gig money were not forthcoming, so he'd thumbed a lift back home to Brentwood from Derby to have it out with his dad. He'd ended up having a blazing row with him and as far as Rick was concerned his father wasn't looking after the band's interest as he should have been.

Rick made it quite clear to us that we're like family to him and he couldn't see us being ripped off. His dad had said all it was was a cash flow problem and it would be all right in the end.

This cut no ice with Rick and subject to our agreement he didn't want his father looking after our interests anymore. He was well upset when he was explaining this to us.

This was a bit of a blow but our respect for Rick had gone up tenfold. We agreed with him that after the tour we'd find ourselves a new manager. He explained that with the weather being so bad he couldn't get any transport to Manchester for the gig. He'd phoned the venue to try to tell us that he wouldn't get there in time, but the geezer on the other end of the phone was well moody and put the phone down on him. We now knew why the promoter was such a cocky little bastard when he threatened not to pay us. Rick added:

'Des had been phoning around to get a number for us. He wanted to thank us personally for sending flowers to the funeral of his Aunt May. I rang him back and I happened to say I was having trouble getting to Manchester because of the snow. He immediately offered to drive me there in his ex-army World War Two Jeep. He said that he and his dad needed to disappear for a bit as the Old Bill were sniffing around their lock-up garage. Something about a couple of Ford Zodiacs they'd supplied to a dealer, both had been cut and shut.'

This brought back memories of the time when I worked for dodgy car dealer Eddie Tucker; he used to do a lot of these cut and shuts, which to the uninitiated is welding two different motors of the same model together. Rick added:

'Within a couple of hours we were on the road to Manchester in this death trap of a jeep. How we won the war with those things I don't know?'

'Where does the tour manager bit come in?' said a grinning Steve.

'I thought I'd give him that title. He was well chuffed with that, he'll do anything for us now.'

Des appeared in the breakfast room of the digs with a massive grin and grease all over his face.

'Do you want to have a look at your new van?'

We all went outside and couldn't believe what we saw. The headlamps and bumper had all been replaced and the van had been cleaned.

'How'd you get all this done?' asked a bemused Tony.

'I always carry my tools in the back of the jeep and I happened to come across another Transit and did a straight swap with their headlights and bumper. Didn't have time to swap the rad over, but I'll be on the lookout for one of them on the rest of the tour.'

'So do we take it that some poor bloke with a Transit has been mugged,' says Rick. 'This sounds like highway robbery.'

'They don't call me Dick Turpin for nothing,' said a sniggering Des.

❧ ❧ ❧

Our next gig was at a working men's club in Bolton, a first for us. We didn't know what to expect, but soon found out. As soon as we arrived at this dingy looking hole, wedged between a row of *Coronation Street* type houses, we were told by the unshaven steward who looked like he'd been on the turps all-night, that within five minutes of playing we'd soon know whether the audience liked us or not. If they didn't it would be a rough ride. He showed us into the hall, a real hovel. The stage was just above floor level and there were wires hanging out of the electrical sockets.

'Is this it, then?' asked Tony, looking unimpressed.

'We had a chart-topping band here last week, they thought this was a top venue,' said the steward.

'Where were they from St. Dunstan's?'

This went completely over his head and he just gave a vacant look, not difficult for him. He disappeared down the cellar while we took the gear out of the van. It was handy having Des on board as he got stuck in with us. After we'd done Des said:

'I'll give the van a spin and sort out a rad.'

'Ok, fine but we don't want the police coming down on us because you've tea-leafed somebody's radiator,' I said.

'No sweat, you worry about playing and I'll worry about the transport. Remember, I'm the tour manager and I get paid for sorting out problems.'

And with that he was off like the favourite at Walthamstow dog track. I said to Rick:

'He mentioned money. Is there something you haven't told us?'

Rick was like the second favourite at Walthamstow as he disappeared into the bog a bit lively.

We rehearsed for about an hour after Tony had sorted out the stage wiring; he'd given the steward a right bollocking about it. With about two hours to go we were introduced to the committee's chairman, another miserable bastard. He then dropped one in and said:

'My son Donald is a great singer and when any band comes here he always sings a few songs with them.'

'Oh yeah, I don't think so, we're not a backing band for a talent contest mate,' said an annoyed Rick.

The chairman's face was a picture and then he got arsey:

'Put it like this, if he doesn't sing you don't get paid.'

'You don't seem to like paying for your acts up north, do yer?' I said and with that he sulked off, but he made it quite clear his son was going to sing tonight.

When he said this we phoned Anthony to ask about payment for this gig. He confirmed that when he deals with working men's clubs he always gets the money up front as they've a habit of not paying if they don't like the acts. This made us feel a lot better.

ã€ ã€ ã€

A little later Des turned up with a twinkle in his eye.

'Job done,' he said, 'And before you ask, the rad ain't nicked. I went down to a scrappy and they had one there. They sell all types of gear, not just motor parts. They were a good bunch of blokes and let me change it over using their ramps. When I was down there I came across one of those foggers.'

'What're you on about, Des,' I said.

'You know, when you're watching *Ready Steady Go* or *Top of the Pops* on the box, sometimes a mist appears on the stage as the band is playing.'

'Oh, yeah, I know,' said Tony.

'Well I've just bought a second-hand one; thought you could use it in your act. You ain't got to pay me now; I'll put it on the bill along with the radiator and my wages. I also got you a wind machine as well; you could use that in conjunction with the fogger.'

We all looked at Rick as if to say you wanted him, you pay him.

ठ ठ ठ

Sometimes you never knew what Tony was thinking. He collared Des and said:

'Can you bring in this fogger you've just bought?'

'I need some help with it, mate,' Des replied.

We were expecting a smallish, plug-in unit. Instead Tony and Des struggled in with this monster of a machine. It looked like it had been nicked off a steam train. It had a steel chassis sitting on a metal block. Looking closer it had a metal tag on it with 8,000 watts stamped on it. This wasn't for a small stage show like ours. This was an industrial job for a large film set or for the fire brigade to simulate a major inferno.

'What are you going to do with that?' said Rick to Tony.

'Don't you worry about that, Ricky boy, it's all in hand.'

Des and Tony manoeuvred this lump of metal to the side of Tony's drum kit and we thought nothing more of it. The punters started to drift in and head for the bar; they didn't give us a second glance. They were here for the beer and we were secondary.

Then this prat came over to us and introduced himself as Donald, the chairman's son. He was about 30 and had tried to make himself look like Elvis. He had long side burns, greasy black hair and an outfit consisting of a ruffled shirt and tight drainpipes that were far too short for him. What a mess, and to cap it all he tried to talk with an American accent:

'Right guys,' he said, 'You know who I am, I want to sing three numbers: Roy Orbison's 'Dream Baby'; 'Rock Around The Clock' by Bill Haley and The Comets; and finally the king of Rock, Elvis, with that great number 'His Latest Flame.' '

He then handed Rick the sheet music of the three songs. Rick was just going to give him some verbal when Tony butted in:

'That's not a problem, Donald, I've heard you're a tasty singer, so of course we'll do anything you want. Can I respectfully suggest that you close the first set with the Elvis number and open the second set with the other two songs. How's that grab yer?'

'That sounds great, sorry, I didn't get your name.'

'It's Tone and I'm the drummer, we can't wait to hear your great voice, Donald.'

As Donald went back to the bar happy as a pig in shit we all looked at Tony.

'Have you just had a handful of purple hearts?' asked Steve.

'Look we know he's a tonker but I've got it all sorted, trust me, have I ever let you lot down?'

'Yes,' said everybody.

With that he disappeared with Des outside the hall for a chat and a roll-up.

๑๏ ๑๏ ๑๏

The 150-odd punters were now in the hall. The men and women sat at separate tables, the women on pints just like the men. Not a teenager to be seen. The Park Drive fags were lit up and the pints of brown and mild were on the table, and now they were waiting for the entertainment.

We stayed with covers, deciding to play safe with some old favourites like, 'Shakin' All Over' by Johnny Kidd & The Pirates; 'Wonderful Land' by The Shadows; and 'Halfway To Paradise' by Billy Fury, my mum's favourite. There was a small dance area in front of us so the ladies could have a dance while the men were getting their pints down their throats. Des was in his element, he played the tour manager to the full, I could see he had his eyes on a couple of the younger women.

We started the set to a lukewarm reception. It helped when Des pulled one of the women off her table and started doing the twist with her, which she seemed to enjoy. One or two others got up and started dancing but not one bloke got up to dance. One of them was getting well pissed off with Des who was now smooching a bit too closely with his missus. You knew it was only a matter of time before he was going to have a word with him. It was now time for Donald to do his party piece. Des quickly left the woman and went over to Tony and sat next to him; they were up to something. For one reason or another Tony wanted to introduce Donald.

'Mr. Chairman, committee, members, ladies and gentle-
men, it's what you've all been waiting for, your very own
Donald who has kindly offered to sing three numbers for you
tonight.'

They all clapped wildly as he stuck out his chest, put his
pint down and slowly walked over to the mic which Rick
grudgingly gave him. Tony continued:

'His first song is that classic Elvis number 'His Latest
Flame.''

We hadn't a clue how to play it but Tony said:

'Don't worry about it, you won't need to.'

So we didn't.

Donald gave a cough to clear his throat and waved to
his fans. He was just about to sing, 'His Latest Flame' when
there was this bleedin' loud bang followed by a whoosh.
The noise was like the feckin' launch of the Apollo rocket.
Des had activated the fogger and the room was now filling
up with mist. Donald screamed down the mic and had now
completely lost it. I quickly turned and saw Des and Tony
crying with laughter. Des quickly turned it off and the mist
started clearing. The old fogger had done its job.

That was the end of Donald's spot on the show; he was
now a broken man. At the end of the first set a few people
came up to us and said he was a crap singer and we'd done the
audience a big favour.

The second set was okay and the committee were happy
with us, except for the chairman whose son was still shaking
after his experience with the fogger. The only downside of the
night was that Des had got too friendly with the woman he
was dancing with. He'd taken her outside in the middle half
of the second set and they ended up in the back of his jeep for
a quickie. Her old man who'd consumed a fair amount of ale

had noticed that they were missing and what followed could only be described as a bit of a punch-up.

After the show we packed up our gear quickly as we didn't want to get involved with any domestic disputes and headed for our next gig in Blackpool.

♪ 10 ♪

From Blackpool to Reading

The only thing good about Blackpool was the rock. We had a real shocker of a gig. Rick had a sore throat and sang like a donkey chewing a carrot. Des offered to sing, but we blanked him. Tony's piles were so bad he was playing drums standing up. I had a couple of blisters on my left hand. It was suggested I'd been using it for something else, but I'm right-handed! Only Steve was up for it, so much so he played lead on a few numbers and I played bass, no wonder it was a bad gig.

We played Liverpool next, then back down to Coventry and on to Gloucester. There was a funny little story that happened in Gloucester. Des is a staunch Englishman, so much so he has a union jack flag flying on his jeep and also outside his house in Romford. While we were there we met some girls. One of them was making a play for Des, but he was ignoring her. She wasn't a bad bit of stuff and could certainly put the lager away. There was one problem for him, she was German. I said to Des,

'Why aren't you chatting her up?'

'I'm afraid, Nick,' he said, 'it's a bit too soon after the war.'

That was that, but she didn't go to waste as Steve had no worries cementing Anglo-German relationships.

We then did a gig just outside Cheltenham. When we arrived there we were told that one of the big Liverpudlian bands was playing at nearby Cheltenham and they weren't expecting too many people to turn up at our gig.

They were dead right, only 24 people showed and five

of them were staff. We still had to do the two sets and be professional about it.

It didn't get any better at Tewkesbury. There were a lot of people at the venue, including a group of girls with their boyfriends; the girls kept smiling at us while we were playing. Of course we were smiling back and enjoying the attention. After the gig their blokes were waiting for us and we had a right punch-up with them. As there were about eight of them and only five of us it was a bit of a problem until Des brought out this ruddy great big sword from the jeep and started swinging it about like one of the three musketeers. He'd had about six pints so he was well tanked up. They ran in all directions, so did we. He was going to get somebody and he didn't care who it was.

On the way to Taff land for the next two gigs we stopped at The Silver Fox, a well-known roadside cafe used by bands in Broad Oak, Gloucestershire. The gigs at Newport and Cardiff didn't go down too well. They didn't seem to be impressed with us or our music at either of the shows. The best thing that came out of Wales for us was their Welsh cakes, they were handsome.

The second part of the tour would be more high profile as the other two bands we were touring with were household names and it would take us to another level. Only one problem, it was now two weeks instead of a month's tour. The agent had told Rick's dad but he hadn't passed the information on to us. We were well sick about this, but two weeks is better than none.

Next stop was Bristol followed by Taunton, Bridgwater, Minehead, Weston-super-Mare and finally for two nights at the Embassy ballroom, Reading. Weston was an afternoon show for a load of students at the college. While we were setting up, one of the girl students, who was quite attractive, came over to us and asked:

'It's my birthday today, would it be possible for me to sing, 'Twinkle' by that girl singer, Terry?'

This girl was behind Rick when she spoke and he said as he slowly turned around to face her:

'How many more times have we got to tell these people we're not a backing band for amateur singers so the answer is ...'

He then clapped eyes on her.

'Yes, of course. By the way, what's your name?'

We all roared with laughter.

Rick did have a thing about people wanting to sing with our band. We first met him at a birthday party for his then girlfriend Andrea. I was a guest singer for the band providing the music on the night. Andrea's singing was so bad she cleared the hall in seconds. Rick felt sorry for her and sang with her. That's how we met. He had a great voice and he joined us right at the start.

As it happened the student had a really good voice. After the gig Rick gave her some coaching lessons! Steve and I also ended up with a couple of girls. Usual problem, they lived with their parents so we couldn't go back to their places. It was a cold night and it was pissing down with rain so we took them to the ABC to see *The Great St Trinian's Train Robbery* which starred Frankie Howerd, George Cole and Reg Varney. After the popcorn, a choc ice and a Woodbine, it was down to a bit of hanky panky in the back row. The trouble is when you're enjoying yourself you make a bit of noise. Both the girls were a bit vocal and there was a fair bit of 'oohs' and 'aahs' and unfortunately some 'nos'. This was brought to the attention of a rather aggressive usherette who kept shining her torch in our direction. She shouted out loudly:

'We'll have none of that in here. If you don't stop what you're doing you'll be thrown out.'

Fifteen minutes later we were out in the street. That was the first time Steve and I had been thrown out of a cinema. The girls had to be home by 11.00 so we went back to our digs for hot chocolate!

❧ ❧ ❧

On arrival at the Embassy ballroom, Reading, we got some really bad news. Rick had taken a call from his mum and came out of the office looking well pissed-off.

'What's wrong mate?' asked a concerned Tony.

'It's the old man. He's been arrested and it looks like he's been banged to rights.'

'What do you mean?' I asked.

'He's been involved in the hijacking of a load of spirits in Ilford. The lorry has been found in my dad's yard.'

It all went quiet until Steve said,

'You're gonna have to go home now, Rick.'

'I know, mum's well upset, and where does that leave the band's finances? It's been hard enough getting money out of him, we've got no chance now. I need to speak to our agent to make sure he doesn't send any more money to my dad's bank account.'

Des said:

'I'll run you home now; it will only take about three hours.'

'We've got a gig tonight, I can't do that.'

'Yes you can,' said Tony, 'we'll get by tonight somehow.'

And with that Rick left with Des. Then Tony said:

'I know it's a long shot but I wonder if Ray of Bad Brakes has a gig tonight? Barnet is only a couple of hours away.'

We tracked Ray down to a bird's house in Tottenham. He had no bookings on for a few days so he was well up for it. He arrived in plenty of time for us to have a rehearsal. We agreed to do the same two sets we did in Manchester.

We got stuck into the rehearsal and the chemistry was still there with Ray. The Embassy was a brand new dance hall and had two bars and a large dance area. We were looking forward to playing there because a lot of the venues were normally pre-war rundown buildings.

We heard from Rick and it was bad news. His dad was locked up in an East London nick and there was no chance of bail. Rick had got in touch with the record company and told them that his dad was off the radar. We told him about Ray and he was well pleased as he wouldn't be able to make it the next night either as he had a lot of sorting out to do. Ray had no problem doing the gig; he was well chuffed to be singing at a large venue like this.

As we walked on to the stage that night a nice cheer went up from the packed hall. We plugged in our guitars, Tony adjusted the top hat on the drum kit and Ray took the Shure mic from the stand. We then went straight into 'Wild Thing' by The Troggs. Midway through the first set I looked out to the audience as we were playing another number. At the front of the stage near me I saw a familiar wave. I was so shocked I missed a chord change and got the evil eye from Ray. Surely it wasn't her.

᾽᾽᾽ ᾽᾽᾽ ᾽᾽᾽

I'd met Anita four years ago when we were playing Exeter. I went for a haircut in Dawlish and she cut it for me. She was engaged at the time, but later we went out together after she broke up with her bloke. She later moved to Reading to live with her sister and I went out with her for quite a while. Well for me it was a long time. Later she jacked me in as I was touring and there wasn't much commitment from me, a really bad move on my behalf.

As soon as the first set was finished I jumped off the stage to talk to her. She looked well tasty with her mousy brown hair modelled on the Mary Quant style.

'Hello, Nick, long time no see.'

'You're still looking lovely, Anita, and you're still wearing Secret de Venus perfume. Every time I smell that I think of you.'

She laughed and said:

'You're still full of it then, nothing's changed.'

'We've got to meet after the gig, we've so much to talk about.'

'As I said, Nick, nothing has changed with you. I can't stop; my friend Jenny has gone to get the drinks. It was nice seeing you again.'

'Have you got a boyfriend?' I said.

'Yes, Simon, and we're hoping to get married one day. It was great to see you.'

As she turned away, I said:

'Is the Tropicana coffee bar still there, where we used to go?'

She stopped and gave me a puzzled look, and replied,

'Well, yeah, Nick, why?'

'Maybe we could meet there tomorrow, say about 10.00.'

'Sorry, I don't think so.'

She moved quickly away and I shouted:

'I'll be there just in case you change your mind.'

I went into the dressing room where the lads were enjoying a beer.

'What happened on that number, Nick,' said Steve taking the piss, 'You lost it big time, lucky I did a nice run on the old bass, in fact it sounded like I was playing lead.'

'Do you know, Steve, sometimes you talk a load of bollocks.'

I stormed out of the room and went outside for a smoke. Anita had really got to me; I don't normally get a cob on about girls. After a cough and splutter I went back into the dressing room and apologised to Steve and got on with the second set. Knowing Anita was out there I played it really cool on the old guitar with an extra few solos. I looked out to the audience a few times but didn't see her again. Ray was having the time of his life fronting the band. He'd brought his bird with him and she was lapping it up. All in all it was a great night. Ray's bird couldn't stay overnight; her parents were having none of it, so after the show he took her back home. He said he would see us at tomorrow's gig.

ঌ ঌ ঌ

At 10.00 I was sitting in the Tropicana enjoying a Pepsi and an Eccles cake. I felt sure Anita would show. I'd put an extra splash of Old Spice on and smartened myself up. How wrong I was, I waited an hour and she never showed. I was kidding myself; she was a smart girl and had moved on. I was still trying to be a Jack-the-lad and had come well unstuck.

ঌ ঌ ঌ

I must admit, I was looking forward to my mum's homemade cooking and to sleeping in my own bed for a few days. I'm not knocking the band life, it's ace, but a few home comforts always go down well.

One of the bands who we were touring with in a few days time had just made the top five in the charts. I hoped we could hold our own with them and wouldn't sound like a Mickey Mouse outfit. We also had the worry of Rick's dad, Mr. B, and whether there was any money left in the pot. To be fair Rick had phoned us up and said he was on the plot, he'd visited our agent and made sure that all monies were being paid direct to us. Ray turned up the following night in plenty of time for a bit more rehearsing and to go over a couple of numbers we hadn't quite got right the previous night.

The gig went really well. I never saw Anita there, why I thought she would come I don't know. As we were off home we said our goodbyes to Ray who was now the unofficial fifth member of the band. He was a real top bloke and hopefully we could work together again soon.

As we were putting the last speaker into the van the promoter, T.J., as we called him, came over to us and said:

'Thanks for two great nights, lads. You really went down well with the audiences.'

We thanked him and I was just shutting the van door when he hurried back and said:

'I nearly forgot, I've been given two notes – one for Steve and one for you, Nick.'

He handed Steve his note and I took the other one. Steve automatically opened the envelope and started reading it. We were always getting notes from people so I just put mine in my pocket. I was more interested in getting home.

Steve then shouted out: 'Listen to this, lads.'

Dear Steve,

It was great to come and watch you play over the two nights. Your bass playing was superb, especially when the lead guitarist messed up on the first show

> *and you took over the lead on your bass. The way*
> *you move on stage is really sexy. Out of all the band*
> *members you are the star.*

Steve stopped for breath and said: 'This bird knows quality.'
He continued:

> *I'm definitely coming to watch you again. I've put*
> *my telephone number on top of the page. It would*
> *be great if you would ring me.*
>
> > *Love and best wishes, John.*

There was a deathly silence until Steve said,

'What's that all about?'

'Well as it happens, Steve, the boys and I have been a bit
worried about you lately.'

'At least my birds turn up to see me.'

I suppose I asked for that after the non-appearance of
Anita. Mind you it didn't stop me and Tony winding him up
all the way back to Romford.

♪ 11 ♪

———— ·❖· ————

A Great Party

It was great to wake up in my own bed with my mum fussing around me. Even though I'd been away she still wanted her £2 a week housekeeping. She brought me up a nice cup of PG Tips and some Marmite soldiers. She'd already started the washing. Unfortunately, with no washing machine she had to do it all by hand. Hopefully once I'd earned some decent money I'd buy her one of those new Hotpoints. My dad's spare cash goes on pints of Double Diamond. As I was getting up she came into the room and said:

'I found this letter in one of your pockets; it's a good thing I checked before I started washing your trousers.'

'Just throw it away, mum.'

'You can't do that Nicholas; somebody has taken the effort to write it, so you should read it.'

I hate being called Nicholas. All the kids at school used to call me bleedin' Nickel Arse. She handed me the crumpled envelope that I had been given at the last gig. As my mum left I read it:

> Dear Nick,
>
> It was nice to see you again at the Embassy. I didn't meet you at the Tropicana as I think we've all moved on since I last went out with you. It would've been unfair to Simon to have met up with you.
>
> Best of luck with the band and I shall always remember the good times we had together.
>
> Love Anita x.

I pondered over the letter and realised how much I still liked her.

೩ ೩ ೩

Steve and I met Rick and Tony at La Nero to discuss the band's future. Rick's dad was out of the frame as our manager. He was still on remand as the police had charged him with a couple more hijackings. Rick was well upset, but kept it to himself; we were there if he wanted us.

The Old Bill seemed to follow us around. Des on his return from touring with us decided he liked this leather jacket hanging up in a clothes shop. He put a brick through the window but couldn't get the jacket off the dummy, so he nicked the dummy as well. He was running down Romford High Street at 2.00 in the morning carrying this bleedin' dummy, when suddenly a cop's car with two coppers on board came out of nowhere and collared him.

The band agreed we'd manage ourselves until we found the right person to look after our affairs. Anthony our agent seemed pretty honest and we felt comfortable with him. The last gig we did was at the new Embassy ballroom. The promoter was so impressed with us he'd booked us for a week. Their resident band was having a break, so we were filling in. It was a good earner and the accommodation was in a hotel, part of the new complex. It fitted in well as we were going to have a few days off after the second part of the tour. We'd sooner have a week's work than be at home. Anthony had also booked us a Sunshine Tour as it was called. We called the tour the three S's, sun, sea and sex. The tour would be taking us to holiday resorts in July and August. There would be plenty of girls about so that was something to look forward to.

The record company had gone a bit cold on us. They were in the middle of a takeover and all bets were off at the moment. They did indicate that everything was fine and for us to keep working on new material to take into the recording studio.

In a few days time we'd be off on the second part of the tour with the two mega bands; we were the support act. We were down to open the first and second sets at each of the venues.

During the short time we had off we all decided to do our own thing. Rick was staying at home to sort out his dad's affairs and help support his mum, while Tony was going down to Great Yarmouth to see Slack Alice again and revisit the beach hut. Steve and I stayed around Romford as we wanted to see a few friends and hopefully find a party to go to.

ત્ર ત્ર ત્ર

About three years ago we'd lost three of our closest friends, Carol, Rod and Jimmy, in a car crash. Steve and I went to lay some flowers on their graves at Crow Lane, Romford. There were tears in our eyes as we looked at the graves and remembered the good times we had. They were part of our group that had knocked around together since we were kids.

As it was Saturday we went and saw the Hammers play Manchester United at Upton Park. Before the game we had pie, mash and liquor from the shop just around the corner from the ground. The West Ham team included Moore, Hurst, Sissons and Boyce. It was not a day to remember if you were a Hammers fan as they got mullered 6-1 by the likes of Charlton and Best.

On the way back we went into La Nero to see what parties were on. We were in luck as Mandy was having one.

She and her mate Viv were two girls that Steve and I would go out with when we had nothing else fixed up. They were the female equivalent of us; if they had no one to go out with they would give us a bell. They liked a good time and could show you a good time. Like us they played the field and never went out with blokes very long. Viv's dad had a stall down Petticoat Lane in East London selling women's clothing. I reckon he was the one that they coined the phrase from, 'off the back of a lorry'. Both girls worked on his stall. They were well Mod and they always dressed in the latest fashions. They both had blonde hair and modelled their hair on the Twiggy look, as a lot of girls did at that time. The bonus was they always wore the full rig, not those sexless tights. Mandy's mum, Gloria, was a bit of a goer, in her forties with dyed blonde hair and a preference for miniskirts. She'd already worn out three husbands. A while back she was in bed with this bloke and he had a heart attack while they were on the nest. She dialled three nines and when the ambulance men arrived she said:

'I didn't know I was that good.'

৵ ৵ ৵

We went home to change before the party. It was mum's night out as well. Dad took her down the Legion every Saturday night. The other six nights he was down there with his army mates playing crib, shove ha'penny or darts. Mum didn't seem to mind as she went to the WI or played whist down the church hall where she still cleaned for the vicar.

My brother Arthur was taking his spotty bird Deirdre out to the Ilford Palais. What pissed me off is that she picked him up in her motor and ferried him about all over the place. As

I mentioned previously I've never had a bird who's owned a motor. He's a cocky little bastard and he was full of himself as he was about to go out, so I said casually to him,

'Do you still get your Johnnies from Sid the barbers?'

All clever like he replies:

'Yeah he gets me the extra large ones.'

'Haven't you heard then?'

'Heard what?'

'Sid's had a couple of bad batches. There's more feckin' holes in them than a colander. I thought I'd just let you know.'

I called for Steve and we were off to the party. All the gang were going so it should be a good night.

ঌ ঌ ঌ

With a couple of tins of Watney's party four we knocked on the door. The door opened and standing there in hot pants with her tits hanging out of a low top was Mandy's mum, Gloria, closely followed by Mandy, who didn't seem too impressed with her mother.

'Look who's here, Mand, it's our pop stars from Romford. Come in boys, which one of you is going to dance with me first?'

We were hauled in; the party was already in full swing with 'Purple Haze' by the Jimi Hendrix Experience blaring out from the Dansette. Most of our mates were there and a couple of Gloria's friends all tarted up for action. Mandy and Viv came over and started dancing with us. Viv was dancing with Steve and shouted out to Mandy:

'I told you he'd come back for more.'

The music went from a fast twist to a slow smooch. Mandy was eating me with the longest snog I've ever had and I hadn't even had a drink yet. Steve was having the same problem with Viv. We finally got away from them and had some Watney's pale ale and a Woodbine. Ronnie joined us; he was the original wide boy.

'How're you going, Nick?'

'Great Ronnie, what're you up to mate?'

'As it happens I was hoping you two would be here tonight.'

'I'm not nicking any more pigs for yer, Ronnie.'

૭ ૭ ૭

A while back, Ronnie had taken me out one night to pick up a consignment of meat for a butcher friend of his. I didn't know he was nicking the meat and it was still alive!

He said he wanted a bit of help with the lifting and there was a nice drink in it for me. We drove to a smallholding in Rainham, kidnapped this pig and Ronnie killed it. Like an idiot I helped lift the porky into the boot of his Ford Anglia but it was too big so we put it on the back seat with a blanket over it. Five minutes later he picked these two birds up at a bus stop and was taking them to Hornchurch. The pig was so heavy it sunk down on the springs. These two birds were sitting on the back seat, unbeknown to them, on top of this pig. Ronnie pulled up sharp at a Zebra crossing, the blanket came adrift and the pig's head was on show with blood oozing from its mouth and its tongue hanging out. I'll never forget the words uttered by the girls as one said to the other:

'What the fecks' that, Trace?'

With a loud scream she yelled:

'We're only sitting on a feckin' dead pig, Di.'

૭ ૭ ૭

'I'm not into animals any more, Nick.'

'Well I'm pleased about that, Ronnie.'

'No, I'm into your market now. Look I wouldn't do it for anybody else.'

Reading from a piece of paper he says:

'I've got a Vex amp, a Fonder guitar, a couple of pedals and a Sore mic for a song.'

'Well sing it then, Ronnie, and by the way you've got it arse about face, it's a Vox, Fender and a Shure mic,' says Steve.

'That's what I said; it's all yours for 50 notes. It's a steal at that price.'

'Probably a steal out of the back of a group's van,' I replied.

'No, it's brand new, still in boxes, trust me lads, I'm your mate.'

Steve snatched the piece of paper off Ronnie and read it. He then started laughing and said:

'Ronnie, where did you get this spelling from?'

'Off the boxes, I'm telling you this is kosher.'

Steve started laughing again:

'Ronnie this gear is Japanese, they're copies, they're crap, and they're worth about a tenner, top whack.'

'No, they're the real thing lads. Would I sell you crap?'

'Ronnie, do we look like we've got carrots on our heads?'

❧ ❧ ❧

'Super Girl' by Graham Bonney starts playing, and super girl Gloria grabs hold of me for a dance. She's an animal and all over me. Her mate Dora does the same to Steve. When you've got a 40-year old woman whose tits are in your face and her hands on your arse it's hard to get away. Fortunately daughter Mandy pushes her mum out the way and takes over the dancing. She's a carbon copy of her mum but with her I ain't complaining. After the dance with randy Mandy, our mate Alec, king of the Essex Mods joins us. He's got beads hanging from his neck, hair down to his shoulders and he's wearing a red, flowered, satin shirt with matching wide-bottom trousers. He's smoking a bleedin' great joint and he's definitely on a mission to another planet.

'Where's all the Mod gear gone? You look like you're going to the feckin' Chelsea flower show,' says a sniggering Steve.

'Don't you like it? I've moved on from being a Mod. That's old hat. Rumour has it that this is the summer of love and peace, and this is what everybody will be wearing.'

'I think Steve and I will stay as Mods, thanks Alec.'

'Take it from me lads; if your band stays on the Mod scene you'll come unstuck. You'll have to re-invent yourselves and then it will be too late to start climbing the charts again.'

We both laughed at him as he went over to his bird also dressed in this weird gear.

The party's now moved up to another level. The decibels have been racked up as 'Paint It Black' by the Stones blares out through the small terraced house. I'm sure the walls are moving from the noise. Next there's a loud hammering on the front door; Mandy opens it and a bloke of about 60 is standing there in his dressing gown.

'Can you turn that racket down, otherwise I'm going to call the police; the missus and I can't sleep.'

Mandy in her diplomatic way tells him to 'piss off' and slams the door in his face.

It's all going downhill now. The booze and pills have kicked in and most of the party goers are off their head. Steve has disappeared upstairs with Viv while I'm trying to do the same with Mandy, but her mum keeps grabbing hold of me; *she's* trying to get me upstairs and I'm having none of that.

Two blokes are having a row about a girl. One of them then throws a right-hander and the other bloke goes sliding across the floor, knocking over the Dansette. In the meantime Mandy's had enough of her mum and gives her a whack; she returns the compliment. Its total anarchy now, and it's time for us to do a runner. Alec shouts out as he is running towards the back door, followed by his bird:

'The Old Bill's outside and they're here in force.'

I rush upstairs and call out:

'Steve, have you finished yet?'

A voice from the bathroom shouts out:

'No I bleedin' ain't.'

'Well you have now, the Old Bill's here and we don't want to be mixed up with this crowd. Drugs and wrecking houses are not on the agenda.'

I push the bathroom door open and Viv and Steve are lying in an empty bath with nothing on. Steve now in a panic puts his clothes back on and we both run down the stairs as the police enter the hallway. We're out the back door, over the fence and running down Dagenham Heathway like a couple of greyhounds.

♪ 12 ♪

On Tour with the Big Boys

I got a call on the Sunday night from Ray to say Bad Brakes had broken up. Their manager had gone bust and owed them quite a few bob; they were also in debt to the HP company who'd funded their music gear. They'd sent the heavies round to a gig they were playing in Edgware, and literally took everything off the stage while they were performing. So with no gear or money they had no alternative but to call it a day, tough break.

We'd enjoyed our few days off and now the four of us were on our way to London to meet up with the two chart-topping bands we were playing with over the next two weeks. Des, who was on bail, was giving us a lift in his jeep. We thought we'd go in style!

These were going to be the biggest two weeks of our lives. It really could take us to another planet and the pop stardom which we craved. To say we were excited was an understatement as we headed for the theatre in London's West End where there was a full day of rehearsing for the first night's performance. Our agent, the promoter and everybody involved in the tour was there. A tour bus for the three bands and two large equipment vans were parked outside. All we had to do was play; everything else was taken care of. This was the big time and we were ready for it. The two bands we were supporting, one from Liverpool and the other from the Midlands, were hero-worshipped by the fans; I wished we were.

As we neared the theatre there were about 100 girls outside the stage door. They screamed as the Liverpool band got out of a flash limo and made a dash for the back door of the theatre.

As Des stopped the jeep in the Strand for us to get out he said, taking the rise:

'I wonder how many screams you'll get.'

As we walked in the front entrance of the venue there were no screams for us, they asked us who we were, and that's fame for you. We felt like a fish up a tree.

Now it was straight down to business. The promoter got over the niceties and said we'd be doing a complete run through of the next night's gig in about an hour. Before that, we went on stage for a quick sound check with the sound engineer. We were playing all our own material so it was a big deal for us to play our music in front of a wider audience.

We hadn't met the other two bands yet, but as we walked on stage to start the first practice set both bands were in the front row, eye-balling us. Strangely enough we weren't too nervous and played out of our skin. After the last number both bands gave us a nice applause which pleased us no end. We then sat down and listened to these mega bands going through their paces. As musicians we didn't think they were any better than us. Of course their songs were much stronger than ours; most of them were chart hits around the world. Their movement and stage presence was something we could learn from. We very quickly realised that we were one lucky band to be on tour with them.

After the rehearsal we met them back stage. We didn't find them big-time Charlies and had a beer with them. We didn't want to get too close in case they thought we were star-struck. One of them was a bit arsey. He was the singer in one of the bands and rated himself; he'd a nasty edge to him which we'd have to look out for. A couple of the others were a bit flash –

why not, when you are top of the pile, earning a fortune and you've got as many girls as you want, who wouldn't be?

❧ ❧ ❧

The next night the auditorium was crammed with girls as we walked on stage to start the first set. We all wore the same union jack tee-shirts, blue strides and baseball boots. We got a fair reception even though we weren't the stars of the show. There were a few screams as we went straight into 'Suburban Mod'. The buzz of the audience was nothing we'd ever experienced before. We were in good form and really put ourselves about on the stage. After we finished our short set we left the stage to thunderous applause. On our way back to the dressing room the concert promoter congratulated us on our performance.

As we were lighting up our fags and uncapping a few light ales there was this volley of screams coming from the theatre as one of the mainline groups hit the stage. What a noise and as Rick said:

'Until we get screaming like that lads we'll always be a jobbing band.'

We opened again on the second set which was only three numbers, so we made them count. Again we got a good reception as we left the stage. To be honest the crowd was just waiting for the Liverpool band to come on. The band got the full works and the screaming was deafening. The big plus for us was that we'd appeared on each of the sets.

After the show all three bands went out on the piss and had a great night.

❧ ❧ ❧

As we criss-crossed Britain with the two bands on the tour bus we had some great laughs. We had one other thing in common besides being musicians, football. This was handy as the three bands had been invited to a Show Business seven-a-side charity soccer tournament, to take place at the end of the first week's touring.

The venues we were playing at were tip-top and it was a fantastic experience to be part of it. What was great was that there was no lugging amps and speakers about or having to set up the gear on stage, it was all done for you. There were roadies and sound engineers, and we stayed at some tasty hotels. We were now living the dream and felt sooner or later we'd be one of the top groups in the country.

The parties after the shows were wild and full-on. Being with named bands on the tour gave us a lot more experience, which took our playing to another level. It was a win win situation which we revelled in. We were full of ourselves after the first week's work.

The charity football match on the Sunday was another story, definitely no harmony between the bands this time round.

♪ 13 ♪

Football & Showbiz Don't Mix

We knew about the football match in advance and had trained with one of our local teams in Romford. If you read *The Sixties Boys* you may remember that both Steve and I had played Senior Amateur football, nowadays known as semi-professional. We were both very competitive and hated losing at anything, especially football. To be part of a showbiz football match was a real turn-on. Tony was a fair goalkeeper and Rick had played park football so we were up for it. We didn't know what to expect as we turned up at the venue.

What a turnout, literally hundreds of people had come to watch. The teams that were playing included the *Daily Mirror* All Stars, the cast from *Z Cars* and *Coronation Street*, a host of well-known DJs, a professional wrestling team, and actors from a number of West End shows. This is where the pecking order comes in to play. The two bands we were playing with were in the Pop Stars A team, and the four of us, plus two roadies and the lighting guy were in the Pop Stars B team, which meant we were the crap, to make up a reserve team, known in football terms as the 'stiffs', which we weren't happy about.

Touring on the first week with the two bands there were a lot of wind-ups about how far the two pop star teams would progress in the tournament, especially from the singer with the attitude problem. He said he'd been on a First Division team's books when he was younger and they wanted him to turn pro. He was full of it and the atmosphere would get a bit heated with the members of the other two bands. They made it quite clear that if we met them we would get hammered. So it was boiling up very nicely.

Even though it was a showbiz tournament it was still very well run and competitive. There was a match programme and the commentary given by a BBC presenter. The pop stars and other well-known faces were surrounded by big crowds wanting their autographs. The pop stars' team looked like they'd just come from a fashion shoot. They were wearing this dog's bollocks of a football kit while our kit was something out of a jumble sale.

A lot of the other teams had a few ringers in the sides, ex-professional players still able to play a bit. The other three guys in our team had played a little bit of football so we were hoping to go as far as we could in the tournament.

Our first game was against the wrestlers. As you can imagine they were big bastards and were putting it about a bit. The other pop star team were on the side of the pitch taking the piss out of us. We quickly went into a two-goal lead, courtesy of Steve's left peg. After that it was one way traffic and we were in the driving seat. With about five minutes to go Steve got his hat-trick and the wrestlers were getting a bit arsey. I was playing in defence with Phil, one of the roadies who had a terrible stutter. Anybody who's played football knows that you cover each other and if you've got the ball you make sure you tell them if somebody is about to tackle you. I had the ball and was looking to play it out of defence when I heard Phil shout out,

'Ma, ma, ma, ma ...'

Next thing I knew I'd been launched by this feckin' 18-stone animal and landed head-first in the mud. As I was laying there Phil finally got his words out:

'Ma, ma, man on you, Nick.'

The piss taking from the crowd and the pop star team was merciless.

ॐ ॐ ॐ

It was fated that we would meet the pop stars in the semi-final of the competition. To be fair they played really well to get there while we struggled against lesser teams. There was a big crowd at the game watching the pop stars play, not us I hasten to add. They were full of themselves, especially the arsey singer who was giving it the big one with his gob.

They'd also slipped in a ringer in the previous round, a young lad from a London first division football club which we thought was out of order. We watched them play their quarter-final match and were impressed with the pace and skill of this young lad. The lad's dad was watching on the touchline and he was full of it, telling us how good he was. As far as I was concerned the lad had to have an early bath if we were going to win the game. When I played senior football I had a bit of a reputation as somebody who could put a hard tackle in, and it was going to be needed today as this lad was going to tear us apart.

The match was 15 minutes each way and within five minutes we were 2-0 down. The young lad scored both goals and was so quick he could catch pigeons. The arsey singer got right on my tits when he came up to me and said:

'I hope the ref's got a big enough notebook to keep count of the goals we're going to put past you.'

I hate anybody taking the piss out of me so when this young lad tried to nutmeg me I tackled him so hard he screamed out in pain and crumpled to the ground. They had to carry him off; he was the first one in the shower with the Palmolive. Steve and Roy the sound engineer both scored one and it was 2-2 at halftime. The arsey singer came over to me and piped up:

'That was out of order, what you did to that lad.'

'On your bike, mate, that was a fair tackle and you're next so watch out.'

We took the lead through Harry the other roadie.

With only a minute to go the arsey singer was coming towards me. I'ed only got me to beat and then he'd got a clear shot on goal. He was showboating as he tried to send me the wrong way. I don't think I've ever tackled anybody as hard as I tackled him. I launched him up into orbit and he fell to the floor like a bag of spuds. He was lying on the ground holding his shin. Then he gives it the big super star,

'Do you know who I am?'

I bent over him and said:

'No, tell me.'

By then both teams were circling around him including the promoter who was worried about his super star.

'I'm feckin' --- of the ---, that's who I am.'

'I'm glad you told us,' said Steve, 'that's made it a lot clearer.'

We won the game and the tournament and got a barrel of beer for winning.

॰॰ ॰॰ ॰॰

I have to say the last part of the tour was a bit frosty as the other two bands were pig sick that we'd beaten them. The arsey singer had a bad limp after that and didn't talk or acknowledge any of us for the rest of the tour. What made it even worse was that our band was starting to get just as much attention as they were. Rick with his good looks and his superb voice was really helping the cause.

As we came to the last show at Manchester we were convinced that with the right management and some strong material we could make it. We had a terrific last night and our confidence was sky high as we played the last number. After a great party lasting well into the morning we had to travel back to Essex to pick up the van and gear and make our way to Reading. We were now ready to take the pop world by storm.

♪ 14 ♪

Love's in the Air at Reading

As we made our way to Reading in the gig van to the sound of Len Barry's '1-2-3' on the radio, we were as happy as Larry. We'd had a great tour except for upsetting the other two bands at the charity football match. Our music had connected with the audiences and our agent Anthony had had good reports from the promoter of the tour. It would hopefully pay dividends in more bookings. After the week's residency we had a week off and lined up a couple of appointments with companies in the West End to see about managing the band.

The record company was next on the contact list. The complex where we were appearing included a bowling alley, hotel and of course the dance hall, a super venue to play. We were really looking forward to playing and staying at a nice hotel on good wages.

On arrival at the venue we were met by the manager whom we only knew as T.J. He was in his thirties, swarthy, well-built and wearing this well-cut Italian suit. He looked like he'd just flown in from Sicily. He made us really welcome and said:

'Nice to see you again, guys. I've flooded the area with flyers and the local papers have picked up on it as well, so hopefully we'll have it full every night. You were great last time.'

After unloading the gear he took us to our rooms. It was a classy hotel, better than sleeping in the van!

Tony intended moving Slack Alice from Great Yarmouth in for the week; he was picking her up later at the railway station. Rick was not himself – he'd lost that bounce since his dad was nicked. He'd gone into his shell and was looking to go back home a couple of times in the week to help his mum and try and keep his dad's business afloat. To be fair his performance on stage was just as good as ever and he certainly hadn't let us down.

The week's work with one day off was going to be interesting. T.J. had told us in advance that there were going to be different themed nights, to include Mod, Rock 'n' Roll, and Motown which was going to be difficult as we only knew three numbers. There was also a Singles and Fancy Dress night. Hopefully for him and us it was going to attract a wide audience locally and beyond. Fortunately we were pretty versatile, but it was going to be a challenge.

ව ව ව

Tony arrived with Slack Alice just before the sound check. To be fair to her she'd lost a bit of weight, the miniskirt was shorter than ever and the top as tight as you could get. I could see Tony wasn't going to get much sleep this week.

Tonight was Mod night, so the dress code was target tee-shirts and pork pie hats. The publicity must have worked as all the tickets had been sold. T.J. came into the dressing room before we went on stage, to wish us all the best. The amount of gold he was wearing, he must've robbed a bleedin' jewellers. He did look a bit of a wide boy and I wondered what other strings he'd got to his bow.

You'd have to have played in a group to know what an edge there is when you go up on stage to play. It's such a great feeling and tonight was no exception. Being a Mod night meant we played plenty of The Who, Small Faces, Kinks, Yardbirds and of course our own material. They had their own dedicated sound engineer so the sound was mustard. It was a top night and everybody seemed to enjoy themselves.

After the gig we went back to the hotel bar where T.J. was the host. What a piss up, we got to bed at about 4.00.

❧ ❧ ❧

The next day Steve, Rick and I went into the town centre to have a look around the record shops. We'd left Tony at the hotel; he was still at it with Slack Alice. The Beatles had just released their new album, 'Sgt Pepper's Lonely Hearts Club Band'. We listened to it in a sound booth at one of the record shops, it blew us away, what a masterpiece. After listening to that you felt like packing it all in. It was nice to see our single in the shop – hopefully there would be an LP of ours in there soon.

❧ ❧ ❧

Tonight was the Singles night. I asked T.J.:

'What type of music do you want us to play?'

'Nothing heavy, I've publicised it as a night for anyone who hasn't got a girlfriend or a boyfriend and wants to meet somebody.'

We couldn't believe it, an hour before we started the place was jam-packed with kids of 15 to old codgers of 50 plus. The music we were going to have to play had to appeal to all ages. All the blokes were on the side of the dance floor waiting for the kick-off. The birds were on the floor waiting for their prince charming to ask them to dance.

As we played the first chord of 'Happy Together' by The Turtles, which we thought was quite appropriate, there was a stampede, a pack of wild dogs raced on to the floor to grab the birds.

After a few more numbers it settled down as everybody found themselves a partner. The ones that were left were the uglies who were struggling, and there were a few.

We'd just started to play a mushy one when I saw Anita to the left of me. She gave that familiar wave. I was so taken aback that I missed another chord change and the number went downhill after that. Thank goodness it was the last number of the first set.

Anita looked great with a skimpy yellow top and short pleated skirt; she had a mate with her who looked just as nice.

Steve can read me like a book and knew when I cocked up the number a girl must have been involved. He saw Anita and her mate and jumped off the stage towards them. I quickly followed.

'Hi, Anita, still looking as tasty as ever, and who's this with you?'

'See you're still full of yourself, Steve. I've warned Jenny about you.'

I joined the three of them and looked at Anita. I was a bit lost for words after the letter she'd sent me. Steve was off the mark when he took Jenny to one side to chat her up.

'I thought you didn't want to get in touch again.'

'Everywhere I go in Reading I see your band being promoted on posters, in the local newspapers; they've even played your record on the radio this morning. It seems I can't escape you, Nick.'

Suddenly, just when I didn't want it, a load of girls came over to us and started to talk to me and Steve. Normally they'd get our undivided attention, but not on this occasion. As Anita turned to go I said:

'Look, sorry about this. After the show perhaps we can have a drink next door in the hotel.'

'I don't think so, Nick.'

'Look it's only a drink. I'll be there straight after the last number.'

&· &· &·

Steve was besotted with Jenny. I can't blame him, she was a class act with her long black hair and a red trouser suit, which looked great on her. He'd made arrangements to see her in the bar after the gig, so hopefully it would be a foursome. Tony was still banging away. Mind you it was taking its toll as he normally does a drum solo to 'Wipe Out' by The Surfaris but that night he had to give it a miss as he could only just about lift the drum sticks.

We started the second set and Steve and I looked out for the girls, but couldn't see them, they'd probably done a runner. Suddenly it all went pear-shaped when there was an almighty punch-up on the dance floor. It was like the battle of the Alamo. It wasn't any of the youngsters but some OAPs; two women in their fifties were knocking shit out of each other. It progressed further when their friends got involved. It was a nasty confrontation as chairs and anything that could be picked up were thrown. We stopped playing, lit up a cigarette and looked on as the bouncers went in heavy-duty; after about 15 minutes order was restored and we started playing again.

Nothing surprised us when we went on tour; we've seen most things happen on a dance floor, but not two women trying to throttle each other. We found out later they were fighting over a bloke. We were glad to finish that night and left the stage and headed for the bar. Steve and I found a table; there was no sign of the girls as we downed a pint of lager in one hit. T.J. came over and said:

'What a punch-up.'

'You can say that again, we should get danger money playing here,' said Steve.

'So should I,' replied T.J., 'They made the Cooper and Clay fight look a non-event. The drinks are on me tonight, lads, you played really well.'

As he left, Anita and Jenny entered the bar. Heads turned as they walked in.

'I'll tell you what, Nick, these girls are stunners, we've got to keep hold of these two.'

'What with our track record, Steve, no chance.'

The two girls saw us and came over. They'd freshened up their make-up and had certainly made an effort to look nice. Steve and Jenny were getting on like a house on fire but Anita and I were just making small talk. Steve could see this and took Jenny over to the bar to get the drinks in.

'It s great to see you again, you look really nice.'

'Thanks, Nick, it's good to see you.'

'I have to ask, why are you here? The letter made it quite clear that you've moved on.'

'I'm asking the same question, Nick.'

Steve brought the drinks over and could see that we were deep in conversation so he and Jenny went over to another table and left us to it.

'Where's your boyfriend tonight?'

'Simon's on a week-long accountancy course in London.'

'Have you known him long?'

'Yeah, look Nick, I'm going to have to leave, I shouldn't be here.'

As she got up to go I put my hand on hers.

'Please stay, look we're just having a drink, there's no harm in that.'

What I didn't understand was that she didn't pull her hand away, she just kept it there.

'Are you still in hairdressing?'

'Yeah, Jenny and I have got our own salon in town.'

'I'm glad it's going well for you. It seems such a long time ago since I came in for that dodgy haircut in Dawlish.'

She laughed and reminded me that when I had asked her to wash my hair, I had put my knees on the chair and leant forward as I used to when my mum washed it as a kid.

'You're doing well with the band, making records and touring with those two top groups. I saw you last week when you played at Swindon.'

'What! You were there, why didn't you come and say hello?'

I was lost for words as Steve and Jenny joined us again at the table. Anita quickly unlocked her hand from mine.

'Jenny and I have got a suggestion. The band's day off is Wednesday, the same day that you close the salon. What about a ride to the coast?'

'That sounds a great idea,' I said.

'You up for it, Anita?' said an enthusiastic Steve, 'Jenny is.'

'I don't know, Steve, we'll have to wait and see.'

The four of us had another drink and about an hour later the girls left. We did suggest getting them a taxi but it wasn't needed as Anita had her own Austin Mini.

'I hope you can make it Wednesday, it would be great to have a day out with you.'

'Look, Nick, my head's all over the place at the moment I'll have to let you know. I'll leave a message at the hotel tomorrow.'

❧ ❧ ❧

I phoned home the next morning, Mum was in a happy mood, dad was taking her for a day out to Southend. I loved my mum to bits; she was a special lady and hadn't had an easy life. Her home in East London had been bombed during the war and she'd had a real tough time like so many others in the country. She'd worked really hard to bring my brother and me up the right way. Unfortunately she failed with my brother! She'd a number of cleaning jobs and also worked for a local greengrocer. Of course dad had done his bit but mum was the star of the show in our family.

As mums do, she warned me about not eating properly and to make sure I got plenty of rest. Then she said out of the blue:

'Nicholas we don't want any extra family members before you get married so make sure you behave yourself.'

I couldn't believe it; she'd never mentioned anything remotely like it before.

ॐ ॐ ॐ

The band had agreed to meet early in the afternoon to learn a new number which was 'A Whiter Shade Of Pale' by Procol Harum, probably one of my all-time favourites. We had a good session and were ready for the night's gig. That was the good news; the bad news was I hadn't heard from Anita about us having a day out the next day. Steve was well happy as Jenny had confirmed she was okay for it. If Anita wasn't coming she would pick him up in her Isetta bubble car and they'd drive down the coast to Weston-super-Mare. He was full of himself as we went to change for the fancy dress gig tonight.

We weren't enamoured having to put fancy dress gear on, but T.J. was paying our wages so we went along with the idea.

Alan was a member of the Essex band 'Quota Plus' in his youth. From left to right are guitarist Dave Buthlay, guitarist Alan Hammond, singer Dave Moore, drummer Brian Rowland and the very tall keyboard player Dave Hughes. (F.W. Tyler)

CHRISTMAS DANCE

WITH THE

YOKAL - BEATS

WINNERS OF S.W. AREA BEAT CONTEST

at CHURCH HALL, SALTFORD

on SATURDAY, 11th, DECEMBER 1965

Admission 3/6   7.30 – 10.30 p.m.

Refreshments available

The Yokal Beats from Keynsham, near Bristol, well known as a top band in the south-west of England. In the photo right, with their winkle-pickers and cool jackets, are from left to right, standing up: lead guitar Neil White, singer Bob Bruton and drummer Tony Pascoe; sitting are rhythm guitar Jim Hunt and bass guitar Bruce Edwards. Below is their 1500 cwt Ford Thames 400E van which transported the lads and their gear around the south-west in the sixties. (Bob Bruton collection)

Rare photographs of the 17-year-old Cliff Richard, taken at Butlin's holiday camp, Clacton-on-Sea on 21 August 1958. Below left he is seen with two members of his backing group, The Drifters: drummer Terry Smart on the left and guitarist Ian 'Sammy' Samwell who wrote Cliff's early hit 'Move It'. Photographed with them are Joan Saunders and her friend Josie. (Joan Saunders collection)

A young Sixties band called Just Us Few are seen here practising at Cellarhead Methodist Chapel, Staffordshire. The line up, from left to right: David Edge lead guitar and vocals, Railton Brockley rhythm guitar and vocals, Stephen Tunnicliffe drums and cymbals and Jeffrey Bell bass guitar and vocals. For such a young band they could play anything from Jimi Hendrix to the The Byrds. (Stephen Tunnicliffe collection)

Fans mobbing the Essex band The Henchmen at a gig in Hornchurch in 1962. In the middle of the photograph, with the white guitar, is the lead guitarist Ron Saunders. (Ron Saunders collection)

(top left) Mods on the plot in Market Square, Dover. The Dover Saints Scooter Club with member Roger Curd, third from the left wearing a crash helmet, are gathered around a Lambretta series 2 with two fox tails hanging either end of the carrier. Note the parkas, a deer stalker hat on the right and a Donovan cap in the middle. The Mods would congregate at Elizabeth's coffer bar and the Rockers met at Pelosi's. (Roger Curd collection)

(bottom left) Mods on the move going up Crabble Hill out of Dover in 1965. A host of headgear can be seen, including a pork pie and a Donovan hat. Also note that not everyone is wearing a crash helmet, which at that time was not compulsory. My good friend Roger Curd is leading the group on the right. (Roger Curd collection)

(below) Rocker Ivan Bluffield sitting on his 1961 Triumph Tiger Cub 200cc. outside his home in Enfield. His brother-in-law Jim Denny is on the back. Note the 1960 Mini in the background. (Ivan Bluffield collection)

(top left) Ivan Bluffield's 1962, red bubble car 350 BMW with air-cooled engine and Isetta left-hand drive, with his mate Stan Brice in front of it on the Great Cambridge Road, Tottenham. Note the lack of traffic. (Ivan Bluffield)

(bottom left) A typical 1960s holiday with the Morris family and Mitzy the dog enjoying the sun at Clacton-on-Sea, with their caravan on the left and Ford Consul MK1. (Christine Hammond collection)

(below) The good old Ford Anglia with teenager Ruth Bruton (née Winter) sitting on the passenger side, sporting a Mary Quant hairstyle. Note the radio on the back shelf which used to slide from one side to another when turning corners. Behind the car can be seen a Mini and a Morris Minor. (Bob Bruton)

(left) 15-year-old Terry Page from Dagenham, sporting a Rocker haircut, smart jacket and slim-fit tie. (Terry Page collection)

(below) Three sixties teenagers with Ivan Bluffield on the right and his mates, brothers Martin and Tony Gale, at Pontin's Holiday Camp, Weston-super-Mare in 1963. Note their pork pie hats. (Ivan Bluffield collection)

Two sixties girls with the dress of the day on a night out at a dance at the Kursal, Southend in 1965. Christine Hughes is on the left, with Jennifer Critten.

(left) Ivan and Jill are typical 1966 teenagers in love, in front of the sea wall at Walton-on-Naze. Note Jill's bouffant hairstyle which was all the rage in the 60s. They had just got engaged; is this why Ivan is smiling or was it because we'd just won the World Cup?
(Jill Bluffield collection)

(right) It's the summer of 1964 with Martin Gale and two girls from South London in front of a luxury coach at the Isle of Wight. Happy days.
(Ivan Bluffield)

Ivan Bluffield on the right with Ken Freeland at Martello Caravan Park, Walton-on-Naze, Essex on one of the camp's fun bikes. Look at the luxury caravans on the right! (Ivan Bluffield collection)

Alan and Christine Hammond in the Summer of Love.

He'd given us some military jackets and a granddad shirt to wear which, as it happens looked the bollocks. Little did we know in a few months' time there was going to be a new wave of music which in many cases changed how bands would dress and act on stage. We weren't putting on the big army boots he gave us; we stuck with our baseball boots. There were two reasons for this, one was, of course, that we liked wearing them and secondly they were rubber-soled. When you're playing at different venues the electrics at these places can be a bit iffy, so if there's any dodgy wiring and electric shocks about at least you've got rubber under your feet. We knew a really nice guy from a band in East Anglia who was electrocuted because of poor wiring at a gig he was playing at.

It was another busy night. We had a ball and played really well. T.J. seemed to have the Midas touch when it came to marketing this venue. He was a real livewire and seemed to know everybody, especially in the music business. The four of us were thinking about asking him to be our manager, but put it on the back burner until the end of the week.

The really good news was that Anita had got in touch and would be coming tomorrow. I was well chuffed about that. They offered to pick us up as we didn't have the van. Rick was going home to see his mum to try and help her with all that was going on in the family. He assured us he would be back to do the other nights. Tony was taking Alice up to London on the train to see the sights, as she'd never been to the capital before.

❧ ❧ ❧

It was a first for me when Anita picked us up at the hotel in her blue Mini. When she changed gears my eyes focused on her miniskirt which rode up every time she touched the gear stick and put the clutch down.

Steve was in the back with Jenny having his breakfast, well it sounded like it. As we made our way to Weston there was no talk of boyfriends or past events, nothing would stop us having a great day out at the seaside. Anita seemed relaxed as we listened to 'You'll Never Walk Alone' by Gerry and the Pacemakers on the radio. We were enjoying a nice chat, not like Steve who was now so much in love his head was laying on Jenny's lap while she stroked his hair with her long, red-painted finger nails. I don't think she would have done that if she'd known Steve had run out of shampoo a couple of weeks before.

When we arrived at Weston we went straight to a cafe and had a full English, well Steve and I did, the girls just had some toast. The four of us were getting on really well and we were hoping it was going to be a great day. A little bit of the romanticism went out of the window when Steve went to the toilet near where we were sitting. About a minute later an enormous long fart which seemed to last forever came from it. The girls and I looked at each other and we fell about laughing. We were still laughing as Steve came back.

'Have I missed a joke?'

'Do you feel better after that, Steve?'

'What, that fart, that wasn't me, it was the geezer in the next trap, wicked wasn't it?'

We went out of the cafe and straight onto the beach. We bought a ball and Steve and I had a game of football while the girls looked on. When we stopped for a smoke I said to Steve:

'I couldn't believe that fart, mate.'

'Tell me about it, I had to leave my boxer shorts there. I'll tell you what Nick, Jenny and Anita are a class act they're a couple of real nice birds. It's a pity we're not the settling down type otherwise I think Jenny would be somebody I could get to know really well.'

'I know what you mean; it's all right for you she hasn't got a boyfriend. Anita is in a long-term relationship and I've got no chance.'

'Take it from me, Nick, she's still got the hots for you.'

Steve took Jenny for a walk along the beach leaving Anita and me sitting on the sands. It was nice to be with her and relax. I tried to get her to open up about her boyfriend to see how strong the relationship was; I really wanted to get back with her again if I could. She didn't want to talk about it and I could see she was feeling guilty being with me, so I didn't take it any further. She told me that she'd opened the salon with Jenny a year ago and it had really taken off. They were looking to open another one sometime in the near future. It came out that her boyfriend Simon was their accountant and that's how they had met. Steve and Jenny joined us and you could see they were loved up as they were acting all soppy.

Next stop was the ice-cream shop. Steve and I had a Lyons Cornish Mivvi which we felt was a bit expensive at 9d each while the girls had a couple of Walls strawberry splits, even more expensive, they were 10d each. Steve and I were going through our pockets to pay for them, bringing out halfpennies and loads of fluff. I couldn't believe it when Steve pulled out an empty Johnnie packet. Fortunately the girls never saw it. While we were fannying about Jenny produced a crisp green pound note from her purse and paid for them, how embarrassing.

We eventually found enough money to buy the four of us a Knickerbocker glory and a milk shake in the Cabana coffee bar. While we ordered, the girls went over to the jukebox and fed it a couple of bob. It was a great selection and included, 'Waterloo Sunset' by the Kinks, 'Matthew And Son' by Cat Stevens and the final one, 'Ever Since You Said Goodbye' by Marty Wilde. When the last number came on Anita put her hand on mine and left it there.

We had an hour left before our journey back and spent it on the beach.

It was a funny journey back to the hotel as there were few words spoken. I think if the world had stopped at this point in time we wouldn't have changed who we were with or what we'd done. If I was ever going to settle down, Anita would be the one and even Steve, who had only known Jenny a few days, was starting to feel the same way.

As we neared the hotel I didn't know how it was going to be left with Anita. I badly wanted to see her again but events were about to take place that would have a profound effect on me. She stopped the Mini outside the hotel and Steve and I invited the girls in for a drink.

As we were all getting out of the car T.J. suddenly appeared looking worried.

I've got some bad news, Nick, your father rang a couple of hours ago, your mother's been rushed to hospital and she's in a bad way. I've organised a car and a driver to take you to the hospital straight away. He's waiting for you.

♪ 15 ♪

The Worst Week in my Life

As I went through the gates of Oldchurch Hospital in Romford I'd never felt so bad in all my life. I quickly made my way to the reception who directed me to a nearby ward. I found my dad, brother and my mum's sister Kitty by the side of mum's bed. My dad, ashen faced, took me to one side and told me with tears streaming down his face:

'Your mum collapsed while she was doing one of her cleaning jobs. I raced straight here from work. The doctors think she might have had a stroke but they're not sure at the moment, she's also had a nasty bang to the head. They're running various tests to see what it could be. They tell me the next 24 hours will be critical; we've just got to hope she pulls through.'

Through the night we took it in shifts to sit by her side. I stayed all night; I didn't want to leave her. I just sat there talking to her and caressing her forehead hoping against hope she would open her eyes.

The next morning I rang Steve from the hospital to tell him about my mum and her condition. He was very concerned as were Rick and Tony. They wanted to cancel the rest of the nights and come home and support me. It was really nice of them but we'd be letting a lot of people down and I didn't want that. I tried to make a joke of it to Steve and said:

'You've always wanted to play lead guitar at a gig; now's your opportunity.'

I spoke to T.J. who had turned out to be a real diamond and very supportive. I said to him I couldn't come back for the rest of the dates. I explained that Steve would take over on lead and asked him if he could draft in a bass guitarist from a local group.

I went back to my mum's bedside but there was no change. I was well pissed off to find my brother had left the hospital. What an arsehole, one day I'll swing for him. My dad asked me to go back home and get some fresh clothes for mum. I flagged a taxi down and went home. I had to phone the greengrocer where she worked as she was supposed to be working there that afternoon. When I told him, I couldn't believe what he said:

'When do you think your mum will be back to work as we are short of staff at the moment?'

He got both barrels and just two words: 'Piss off.'

I was just about to close the front door and get into my Cortina when the phone went. My heart missed a beat and I felt physically sick as I gingerly picked it up.

'Nick, its Anita, how's your mum I couldn't sleep all night thinking about you and your mum and what you're going through.'

She was just what I needed at that moment. We only had a quick chat as I wanted to get back to the hospital. I said how much I had enjoyed our day out and perhaps we could see each other again. I asked her for her phone number but she was reluctant to give it to me so I backed off. It was left that she'd give me a ring.

❧ ❧ ❧

There was no change in my mum's condition. Dad was knackered, like me, he hadn't slept for well over 24 hours. I had a word with the doctor and he indicated it was a waiting game and if there were any developments he'd call immediately. My tosser of a brother turned up with that slab head of a girlfriend Deirdre; she looked even weirder than ever with her dyed red hair and a long, flowered dress that looked like a smock. Hope she's not up the club – that would finish mum off.

I called Steve later and after we chatted about my mum he said:

'We've got a bass guitarist courtesy of T.J. He's playing tonight, hopefully he fits in. I have to be honest I'm shitting myself playing lead.'

'You'll be ace, mate, you'll have them rocking in the aisles.'

'I hope so Nick; by the way did Anita ring you? I gave her your number.'

'Yeah it was nice to hear from her but she wouldn't give me her phone number which was a bit of a blow. Is Jenny coming to watch you play tonight?'

'Yeah, I've fallen for her big time, Nick. I'd better go as the bass player is coming soon and I want to go through the sets with him. I'll keep my fingers crossed for your mum. By the way the boys send you their best.'

After a couple of hours rest I went back to the hospital and sat by my mum's bed all night. The next morning I went home for a wash and something to eat and to pick up dad.

As we entered the ward a doctor rushed over to my dad and said:

'The nurse has been trying to get you on the phone Mr. Sheldon; your wife has regained consciousness.'

I went into my mum's ward and there was Des with the biggest bunch of flowers I've ever seen in my life, sitting with my mum. How he got in the ward I don't know, as only family members were allowed. He was holding my mum's hand as she whispered weakly to him:

'They're lovely flowers, Desmond, you did buy them?'

'Mrs S, how can you say that, you've known me since I was a kid.'

With a weak grin she replied:

'That's why I asked.'

The prognosis was that my mum had had a stroke, which had made her fall. In doing so she had knocked her head quite badly. The doctors said she was not out of the woods yet, but hopefully they might be able to release her from hospital in a few days time. When she went home she was going to need lots of TLC. I said there was no way she was going back to do all those cleaning jobs and work for that poxy greengrocer. I was going to have a strong word with my old man about the amount of money he was spending down the Legion with his mates. That money would be better spent looking after mum and making sure she ain't got to bust a gut again.

Later that day I got a phone call out of the blue from the record company. They wanted us to go and see them on Monday morning. There was a coolness about the phone conversation which I felt uneasy about.

I phoned Steve and told him to tell the other lads. He said the gig last night went well and the bass guy did okay.

୬ ୬ ୬

My mum was still in hospital as the four of us made our way to London in my Ford Cortina to see the record company. The other nights went well without me so we hadn't let anybody down. T.J. had sent my mum some lovely flowers as did Steve, Rick and Tony which was much appreciated.

I hadn't heard anything more from Anita so that looked like that wasn't a goer. Steve was still feeling strong about

Jenny and he was hoping to go down and see her during the week. We now had a week off before we started the Sunshine Tour.

When we arrived we were shown into an office, and waiting for us there was an American bloke aged about 40. He had slick black hair and looked a slime ball. We took an instant dislike to him. Johnny Curtis, the A&R man, was sitting next to him saying nothing.

The American got up from his chair, went over to the window, looked out, then quickly turned to face us.

'There's no easy way to say this but unfortunately we're going to have to drop you from our portfolio.'

The four of us looked at him not fully understanding what he meant.

'What do you mean, portfolio,' said a confused Rick.

'It means that our investment in your band has now been terminated.'

'Are you trying to say that you are kicking us into touch?' I said.

'Well, yes, our involvement with your band is now at an end.'

'We've got a contract with you,' said an angry Tony.

'Yes, you have, but the contract clearly states for one record only, after that we decide whether we will pursue any further interest in you until the contract expires. If you look at the small print it's made quite clear, your manager should've pointed this out to you. Perhaps that's why he's not your manager anymore.'

'I really don't know where you're coming from,' said a really annoyed Rick. 'Our record got into the top 30, isn't that a result?'

'I'm afraid it's not. Johnny, please explain why.'

Johnny got up from his chair and walked around the room as he didn't have the bottle to look at us straight in the eye. After a coughing fit he said:

'It's like this. Yes you did get in the top 30 but unfortunately it didn't generate enough revenue for us to fund you long-term. Your type of music has a strong Mod influence, this is not what we're looking for now. There is a new era of music on the horizon and our company is going to be the front runner, we've got the bands in place to attack this market.'

'I don't buy that,' said Rick. 'We can play anything you want.'

'It's called originality,' said Johnny, 'You're a Mod band and that's what you're known as. Time has moved on. We're now into a completely new mode of music.'

'What's that, then', said Tony.

Smugly he replied:

'If you were a progressive group you would've seen the change of music that the youngsters want now.'

'Have we missed something, because I don't know what you're on about,' said Tony.

The Yank then piped up:

'Look your band is now old hat, you're good at what you do but you're not for us anymore.'

After that the conversation went downhill. He was taking the piss and nobody did that to us. I went up to Johnny and eyeballed him.

'You think you're so clever. I'll tell you what, Johnny boy; you look at our faces and remember us. We will hit the big-time and we'll come back and haunt you and that wanker sitting over there.' The Yank butted in:

'There's no need for threats.'

Steve went over to him and with a coldness that is unlike him said:

'There's a right way and a wrong way to tell people you want to dispense with their services. You and your mate Johnny have got no class or respect. As Nick said, we'll be back and we'll have the greatest pleasure in proving you two wrong. Remember the name Modern Edge.'

≈ ≈ ≈

As we made our way home the silence was deafening. Every swear-word known to mankind was being uttered under our breaths. We all had our own thoughts about what had just happened. Being bombed out by the record company had shattered our dreams. It's hard enough getting a deal, especially with your own material. To have it snatched away from us was heartbreaking. One trick pony came to mind.

None of us wanted to talk about what had happened, so we agreed to meet at La Nero first thing in the morning to plot our next move. I went to hospital with Steve to see how mum was, she was a bit better, but I was worried about who was going to look after her when she got home. I would, of course, when I was there but with a tour about to start it was not going to be easy. Fortunately her sister Kitty lived around the corner. They were close so I knew she'd be there for her.

I gave our agent Anthony a bell, he didn't seem too concerned, he had bookings for us for the rest of the year. That was good; at least we'd have an income for the next few months. He said he couldn't understand why they had released us, but that was the music business. He also said that he would keep his ear to the ground to see if he could find any other opportunities for us with another company.

≈ ≈ ≈

The next morning we met at the coffee bar. Even our favourite haunt had problems. Ted, the guv'nor, had banned this Rocker from coming in, so he'd put a brick through the window.

As Rick, Steve and I sat down with our espressos Tony walked in with Slack Alice who went to get him a coffee. I'm afraid the conversation went downhill after that. I said to Tony:

'Do you have to bring her here today?'

'She's my bird, we're in love.'

'Every time I look around she's there. It's like having a monkey on your back,' said Steve.

Slack Alice brought the coffees over, grunted, then sat in a corner on her own.

'Tony, besides grunting and opening her legs does she do anything else?'

Tony was just about to climb over and lamp Steve when Rick announced:

'Look, lads, I'm sorry to say this but I'm going to have to pack the band in.'

It didn't register at first, then I said:

'Say that again, Rick.'

'I can't go on. It's nothing to do with the record company; it's just that with my dad on remand my mum can't cope. She's running his transport company with dad's brother but he's got his own problems. I need to take time off to help her.'

'But we've got the tour in a few days time, we can't just jack it in,' says an alarmed Tony.

'I know, I feel really bad about it.'

Slack Alice crept over and asked Tony:

'How long are you going to be, Tone?'

'Oh, piss off Alice, we've got major issues here.'

That was that, she was off, not to be seen again.

'Is there any way around this, Rick, can we help?' I said in desperation.

'No, not right now. Dad's in court soon. I'll know more then.'

'Well, there's always a place in the band for you,' said Steve.

Tony and I both endorsed what Steve had said. The three of us couldn't imagine playing without him.

We looked at every angle to see if there was any way round it, but unfortunately there wasn't. Rick said he'd bring the gig van round to my house later. We talked a few minutes more but it was no good. We fully understood his predicament; he was a mate and always would be. We'd played together through thick and thin for four years and now it had ended because his old man was a crook. He'd a lot to answer for. I know blokes are not supposed to cry but I have to say there were tears in all our eyes as he left La Nero.

We were in real trouble now. After Rick's bombshell we all felt like packing it in, but as they say, the show has to go on. We now had to find a singer who could come on tour with us at short notice. Ray of Bad Brakes fame was our front runner. We agreed to meet round my house that night to see if any other names could be added to our list.

I phoned Ray's house and spoke to his mum who told me he was now singing for a resident band at a holiday camp in Jersey. It was getting worse by the minute. She gave me the phone number of the camp, but he wasn't there so I left a message for him to ring me.

The house felt empty without mum. Dad had gone back to work and hopefully she would be coming out of hospital in a couple of day's time.

As I was drinking a cup of tea my brother Arthur walked in. I felt he was rather blasé about our mum being in hospital and didn't really seem to care too much. I said to him:

'I'm away for a bit soon and I want you to make an effort to help her when she comes out of hospital. On my days off I'll be coming back to do my bit.'

'Look I've got a busy life with Deirdre and I can't see me doing much to help. Dad and Aunt Kitty will have to do most of it.'

'I can't believe you've just said that.'

'Well I'm only telling you how it is.'

He started to walk away from me. He'd only gone a couple of feet when I got hold of him and landed one on him. It seemed to have done the trick, when he said:

'Don't worry, don't worry I'll do my bit, Nick, I promise.'

I know I shouldn't have hit him but he had to know that I meant business. If you can't help your family when they need you then as far as I'm concerned you ain't family.

ॐ ॐ ॐ

Steve and Tony came round to my house to discuss our next move. Rick had brought the Transit round earlier. He was really upset and we had a long talk. He gave us all the paperwork concerning the band including the contract with our ex-record company, which was now only fit for the bin.

Steve had had a word with his dad Tom. He'd offered to look after the band's books and liaise with the agent about our fees and future bookings. He was a solicitor's clerk and had an air of authority about him, unlike Rick's dad; he was stonewall and one of your own. Tony and I readily agreed it would bring some order to the band.

Steve was off to see Jenny for a couple of days. He was also going to see T.J. about maybe becoming the band's manager. I told the lads about the phone call to Ray and that we were waiting to hear back from him.

Arthur came sulking down the stairs with his cranky bird Deirdre. She gave me the evil eye about whacking him. He came into the room and said:

'I'm off to see mum.'

'Give her my love and tell her I'll be in later to see her. And oh, don't tell her about the little accident you had earlier. Don't want her worrying.'

'I will,' said Deirdre. 'That was thuggish what you did to my Arthur.'

'I wouldn't do that Deirdre,' I replied. 'I believe your parents are God-fearing people, in fact isn't your dad the verger down All Saints Church in Rainham?'

'What's that got to do with anything?'

'Well they wouldn't be too happy to know that their only daughter is humping her boyfriend at Upminster Common most nights in the back of her Morris 1100. I'm sure they didn't buy it for you as a passion wagon.'

'You wouldn't?'

'Try me.'

'You're evil.'

They left the room, I could hear them arguing as the front door slammed.

'That was a nice bruise he had, Nick.'

'Little shit, he was owed that, Steve.'

The boys were just about to go when the phone went, it was Ray. I explained to him where we were coming from and about him joining the band full-time as the singer. He was well interested and said he would ring me back the next day with an answer.

❧ ❧ ❧

Things were starting to pick up. Mum was out of hospital and at home. It would be a long job but it looked like she would be okay with plenty of rest and support.

Ray got in touch, and said yes, he wanted to join us. He had to give a week's notice to his band so he'd miss the first gig in Clacton. He was a top lad so we were well happy he was joining us. A lot of bands put the new member on a wage when there's a change of line-up. We didn't believe in that, Ray went on a full percentage, the same as us.

Steve came back from seeing Jenny. He'd seen Anita and she sent her regards. I was hoping for a bit more, but it was not going to happen. Steve had spoken to T.J. about becoming our manager. Unfortunately with the Embassy ballroom he was too busy and wouldn't be able to give it his best shot, so that was a no, no.

Tony had been busy. He'd checked all the amps, speakers and mics and made sure that everything was tip-top. Des had taken the Transit and given it a good service. There was a price to pay, he didn't want any money for doing it but wanted to join us on parts of the tour, starting with Clacton. He was a character and could bring some fun to the party, so he was in.

Steve's dad had come around to see me while Steve was away and we sorted out all the band's paperwork. He'd even been to see our agent Anthony to make sure everything was in place and he was now the contact. This enabled us to concentrate on the music.

We still had to find a manager and another record company, which wasn't going to be easy. At least we had enough work till the end of the year.

So we're now in July and off on the Sunshine Tour. All those wonderful exotic British holiday resorts to visit, first stop Clacton-on-Sea, what more can I say!

♪ 16 ♪

The Sunshine Tour

It certainly wasn't the Sunshine Tour when we hit Clacton-on-Sea, Essex. We arrived at the venue in the middle of a storm, the rain was pissing down. The venue was just off the seafront. We got there really early as we thought we'd have a walk down the prom and see what talent was about. The only things about were ducks and seagulls.

When we got there the owner and his staff were up to their knees in water. There was a leak in the roof and water was cascading down into the large foyer and seeping in to the hall.

'Do you want some help, mate?' I said.

In a strong London accent he replied:

'That would be brill, lads, scoop the water up in the buckets and throw it down the drain by the front door.'

Des said to the guy who was now looking desperate,

'Got a ladder, guv? I'll get up on the roof and see what's causing it.'

'Cheers mate, it's out the back in the shed. I've phoned for a roofer and a plumber. They're so laid back down here, the hall will be floating out to sea before they turn up.'

We were bailing out the water the best we could when Steve nudged me and pointed to a couple of girls who were doing the same as us and said:

'That's the first time we ain't spotted knickers on show.'

He was right, both the girls who were a bit older than us had their skirts hoisted up so they wouldn't get wet, and they'd tucked them into their knickers. After that we couldn't take our eyes off them. About ten minutes later the water coming in from the roof suddenly stopped. Des came in looking like a drowned rat. He went over to the guy and said:

'I've fixed it temporary for yah. You've got three broken tiles and a bird's nest, which I've removed; it was blocking the down pipe. You need to get a roof tiler in to fix it.'

'I owe you big-time. My business partner and I have come down from London and bought the lease and tonight's our first booking. We need every penny to get this place up and running and recoup some of the money on our investment. But looking at all the water in here that's not going to happen tonight, I don't think.'

'Give me a couple of hours,' said Des, 'and we'll be up and running.'

He disappeared and we continued bailing out and looking at the girls' black knickers. We stopped while the girls made us a cup of tea, Geoff the owner looked a worried man as the water level didn't seem to be going down.

Crash, the front door flew open and the cavalry came in, in the shape of Des wheeling this massive pump attached to a large coiled pipe. He started up the engine which sounded like a tank, and put the pipe in the water. The suction was brutal and within half an hour the foyer was cleared of water.

'Where did you get that from, Des?' said a relieved Geoff.

'Well everybody out there has got the same problem. The sudden storm has brought out all the generators and loads of premises are being pumped out.'

'Yeah. But where'd you get the generator from, Des?' I asked.

'I can see you've been enjoying a cup of a tea and so have others. That means they'd left their pumps unattended, so I borrowed one.'

'That means you've nicked it.'

'No. I've borrowed it for a couple of hours, Nick, that's all.'

'Where did you borrow it from?'

'Christ, Nick, you should get a job as a copper. There's a church just around the corner and they've got a water problem as well.'

'Don't tell me you've nicked it from a church, Des.'

'Look, it's Monday today, Nick, they won't need the pews till Sunday!'

❧ ❧ ❧

The dance went ahead and Geoff was well happy. It was a good night and the place was full. Just being the three of us caused one or two problems. We certainly missed Rick out in front.

Des in lots of ways was our saviour. In the morning he was picking up Ray off the Jersey ferry at Weymouth and driving him down to the next show, which was two nights at a holiday camp in Margate.

That night Geoff took us to a real dive after the show and funded the evening. It was his way of thanking us for saving the night. The strippers on show had seen better days but we had a great night and got absolutely wrecked. I'm afraid to say all three of us ended up with girls who you couldn't take home to mum for afternoon tea. The next morning Steve had a real guilty conscience when he woke up and saw the road accident lying next to him.

On our way to Margate we popped into my house for a cup of Camp coffee; Tony actually liked the stuff. Mum was in bed but feeling better. The stroke had left her speech slightly impaired but it wasn't too bad. Her sister and the neighbours were looking after her so I felt a lot happier plus dad had gone from going seven nights a week down at the Legion to five; well it was a start.

As we left for the next gig Tony and I were really giving Steve some stick about the bird he'd bedded the night before and what impact it would have on his relationship with Jenny when he told her.

'Leave it out, I ain't telling her anything. I'm not married to her,' he said.

He was really wild and decided to get his own back. As I was driving through the Blackwall Tunnel there was a loud bang like a gunshot. I nearly crashed the van. There was Steve with a big grin on his face sitting in the back with a cap gun. I could've killed him there and then.

❧ ❧ ❧

When we arrived at the holiday camp Ray was already there. It was great to see him again. There was more good news, he'd split up with his girlfriend which meant he wouldn't be a party pooper. Two days at a holiday camp, that had to be good news on the crumpet front. There was only one thing that we didn't have in common. He smoked these menthol cigarettes which were like smoking a peppermint.

The 1950s-style holiday camp was a bit of a dump. They showed us our chalets; they were bog basic and not very clean, but they were free and so was the grub so we didn't complain.

We were playing that night so unloaded the van and set up. The stage was massive – we'd look like midgets when we played on it. With Ray on board we needed to get stuck in to rehearsing the numbers we were playing.

After a good practice session we went into the camp's restaurant. It certainly wasn't Michelin star quality. The food was just about eatable but it didn't stop us having double helpings with Des having three. Being on the road you took every opportunity when there was free nosh. Normally it was fish and chips, a burger or a mouldy cheese sandwich. It also gave us the time to look at what birds were on show. There seemed to be plenty about, so things were looking up on that front.

Ray couldn't wait to get out there and do his stuff. He had a knack of getting the punters in the crowd to sing which always went down well.

⁂

There were a fair few people in the hall the first night. It looked like it was going to be a good gig when we started playing. Halfway through the first set Ray got the holidaymakers singing along to 'Funny How Love Can Be' by the Ivy League. We stopped playing and as I was wiping my sweaty hands with a towel Steve said to me:

'Look who's here, then.'

Straight in front of us with great big grins and waves were Pamela and Sheila from *Tirpitz* fame; I was so happy to see them. Ray come over to me and said:

'Don't you think it's about time we played the next number? The singing is finished.'

I had completely lost the thread.

The last number most nights on this tour was always 'Summer Holiday' by Cliff Richard. The crowd always sang with us and it was a great finish to the evening.

After the gig we met up with the girls, they were as pleased to see us as we were them. We took them to one of the bars and had a drink.

'How'd you know we were playing here?' I said to Pam.

'Sheila's brother works here as a stagehand. He lets us know what bands are appearing. As soon as we knew it was you we booked up two nights in one of their mobile homes. He gets us a special rate.'

'But you only live in Ramsgate, that's just up the road.'

'Well, chance to see you and get away from our parents.'

This was getting better by the minute. We stayed in the bar with the girls for another hour, but were itching to get an invite back to their mobile, which didn't seem to be forthcoming. Steve and I both gave big yawns and stretched out our arms like we were ready for bed, but it appeared they weren't. I took the bull by the horns and said to Pam:

'It's been a long day so I suppose it's time for bed.'

'Well it was great seeing you, maybe we could meet up tomorrow,' replied Pam.

That was the end of that; they didn't even let us walk them back to their place. As we walked back to our pit Steve said:

'I'm impressed with the way you handled that, Nick. The chat-up line really worked!'

❧ ❧ ❧

Next day, we met the girls and took them to Dreamland, an amusement park in Margate. It was like being a kid again. We went on the wooden Scenic Railway rollercoaster which opened in the 1920s. The Octopus, Sky Wheel, Dodgems, you name it, we went on it. It was a real fun day and we enjoyed being with the girls. But with the fun there was also work to be done. We'd agreed with Tony and Ray that we'd all be back at the camp by 4.00 for some more rehearsing. We agreed to meet the girls after the show, but we weren't sure we would actually turn up as Steve and I didn't like the thought of going to bed on our own.

Tony and Ray were in high spirits as they'd both pulled. Tony was looking after his stomach as the girl he'd met worked in the kitchens. You could tell that as she looked like she'd tasted all the food before it was served to the holidaymakers, she was a size. But Tony liked them big and buxom. Ray got acquainted with the projectionist who worked at the camp cinema; she was about ten years older than him and looked like she'd seen a bit of action in a previous life.

It wasn't one of our better nights for playing, we were all over the place and to be fair it was probably down to me. For whatever reason I was playing really crap, I wasn't concentrating as much as I should've been. That meant more practising, a gentle reminder that you ain't as good as you think you are.

We met the girls afterwards with little enthusiasm as we weren't expecting to get anywhere. At the end of the evening we did the usual yawn and Steve said to Sheila:

'Would you like us to walk you back to your mobile?'

'That'd be nice,' replied Sheila.

We had to stop ourselves running there, we played it cool, and lazily walked the 300 yards back to their place. On arrival Pam said to me:

'Do you want to come in for a coffee?'

'That sounds great.'

We were through that door as quick as a flash. The evening progressed at a pace after that. It was a large mobile so I wouldn't be able to hear Steve huffing and puffing all night. This was just what the doctor ordered as we were about to enjoy our night of passion. There was just one dampener; there was an army of seagulls on top of the mobile all bleedin' night. They were noisy bastards and wouldn't stop whatever they were doing. Steve and I banged the ceiling a few times but within seconds they were back marching up and down on the roof. If you've ever stayed in a caravan or a mobile home when it's pissing down with rain you know the noise. It was like that but ten times worse.

The next morning we said our goodbye to the girls. On the ground outside there were bundles of Wonderloaf wrappings. We looked up at the roof and saw the seagulls enjoying a breakfast of sliced bread. On one of the windows was a piece of paper which read:

'Looks Good. Tastes Good. It's Wonderloaf.'

'Bastards. It's either that Tony or Ray who've done us up?' I said to Steve.

As we walked back to our room we both burst out laughing and Steve said:

'They must've been out all night feeding those poxy seagulls.'

Before we left we'd borrowed the girls' box Brownie 127. They wanted some photos of the band which they certainly got. We returned the camera after taking the pictures; wait till they take them to be developed!

ৡ ৡ ৡ

We met Tony, Ray and Des for breakfast and I knew it was Ray who had set us up when he asked:

'Have a good night listening to the birds, lads?'

Then he told us what he got up to that night, it was really funny. As mentioned, his bird Bev was the projectionist in the camp cinema. Ray went into the back room of the cinema where Bev was running the late film for the holidaymakers.

They both felt a bit frisky and were having a bit of a feel around. Bev obviously wasn't keeping an eye on the projector, as the film came off the reel, tore in half and curled up on the floor. Bev panicked and pushed Ray into a cupboard because she knew what was going to happen next. The door swung open and her unhappy boss asks why this had happened. The holidaymakers had got the cob on as the film was just getting to the exciting bit. She apologised to him and said she'd get it up and running straight away. After he left, Ray came out of the cupboard and between them they spliced the film and put it back on the reel.

Bev started running the film again and the two of them got back to more important matters. Suddenly the door swung open again and her boss shouted out:

'What the hell are you doing, girl? You've put the film back on upside down and the customers are going mad out there.'

ﺽ﮲ ﺽ﮲ ﺽ﮲

After the Margate gig we're about to travel to Brighton for a one-nighter. Des has gone home as he has to go to court regarding the runaway mannequin which happened to have a £20 leather jacket attached to it.

Before we leave we have to sort the gig van out. It's now a health hazard and the smell emitting from it is something else. When you think about it, we've slept in it, ate in it, shagged in it, puked in it and crapped in it. You name it, it's happened in it. We dig out knickers, skid mark pants, porn books, Beanos, rotten sandwiches, half-eaten burgers, fag packets, empty Johnnie boxes. We think we've cleaned everything out when a mouse pops his head out of a packet of mouldy crisps. I don't know who is more frightened.

We don't like paying for diesel; well it's expensive, ain't it? On the camp they have their own fuel pump for their vehicles. The guy in charge is a young lad, nice enough, but fourpence short of a shilling. We get talking to him when he comes up to us on stage during rehearsals. He thinks he's a bit of a singer so we let him have a go in the empty hall. He is so bad I feel sorry for him because he really thinks he is the DB. Once we found out he was in charge of the fuel pumps on the camp we told him he had the potential to be a great rock singer and we'd introduce him to our agent. He's all singing and dancing after that and can't do enough for us.

With a nice tank full of free Cleveland diesel and a sparkling new van we're off down to the south coast. As we're listening to 'See Emily Play' by Pink Floyd on the radio it's obvious the music industry is changing and perhaps our style of music is past its sell-by date. Had we had our eyes closed about the changes that were going on? The question has to be asked, do we just want to be a jobbing band and earn a few quid and have some great laughs, or are we really serious about changing our image and perhaps having another shot at the charts?

I look at Steve, Tony and Ray; like me they are listening intently to Floyd. I wonder if their thoughts are the same as mine. Our life is making music and getting paid for it. How bad is that? As musicians we're as good as most and always give it our best shot at the gigs. Alec our Mod mate had been on the money when he spoke about the change of music. It's the summer of love and the start of the psychedelic era of music which seems to be coupled with LSD, a hallucinogenic drug that takes you to another world or as somebody said a mind-altering experience. I think I'd rather have a Woodbine and pint of Double Diamond.

My thoughts are shattered when Steve does a right across a main road and says:

'Nosh time, lads.'

The van virtually leaps into the car park of a transport cafe, clipping a wall and coming to a violent stop.

❧ ❧ ❧

The Brighton gig was a fantastic night. The management were top people and made us really welcome. The crowd who turned up were in a real party mood and it was one of our better gigs.

It was a nice one for Ray as he'd got his first pair of knickers thrown at him. When the light blue knickers hit the stage he looked over to the girl who'd thrown them. After the first set he jumped off the stage and went straight over to her and returned them, that was him sorted for the night. She had a mate with her and Tony was on her case. After the gig we never saw them till the following morning, just before we left for our next job at Hastings. Steve and I were a bit choosy, too choosy as we met nobody and just got tanked up instead.

If Brighton was a great night, Hastings was an absolute bleedin' nightmare.

♪ 17 ♪

The Battle of Hastings

If we thought we were heading for the big time when we turned up at the grubby little building called City Hall at the back end of Hastings, then a reality check was due. This certainly wasn't a star venue; you wouldn't put this on your CV. It was a dive and our booker Anthony hadn't come up trumps with this one.

We were a bit early and couldn't get into the hall till about 5.00. In the town there were loads of Mods and Rockers flying about on their Triumph motorbikes and Lambretta scooters. There was an uneasy feel about the town with all this going on. The Mods and Rockers problem was at its zenith in 1964; by 1967 it wasn't so prevalent or at least that's what we thought.

We kept out of the way and spent a few hours on the beach getting a bit of sun on our backs. We were chatting to a few girls, and I don't know how the subject came up but Steve said to this girl:

'What's your dad do for a living, then?'

'Oh he's got a good job, he's a plater.'

Well we rolled up; she couldn't see what was so funny about it until one of her mates told her.

'That's disgusting. Is that what you Essex boys are like?'

It was now time to return to the hall and get ready for the gig. As we entered the car park we recognised Des's jeep. He came bounding over to us and Tony said to him:

'Why aren't you banged up?'

'You won't believe this. The leather jacket that they reckoned I nicked ...'

'Hang about Des, you did nick it.'

'Not in the eyes of the law, Tone. Would you believe the police had lost the evidence? My brief Mr. Goldstein stated to the court that without the said jacket the charge should be thrown out of court and it was.'

'You're kidding.'

'Tony, would I embellish the truth?'

'Yeah, bleedin' right you would. I still don't believe it, but you're here now and we're pleased to see you, now get your arse in gear and help us unload the van.'

ॐ ॐ ॐ

Nothing about the booking felt right. The guy who was running it didn't seem too interested in music or the gig, so he couldn't have been the owner. It was his job to be there and oversee everything and that's what he was doing.

The hall held about 150 people. It was run down and looked like an original flea pit. Windows were broken, it was a pigsty. The cisterns in the toilet were hanging off the wall. We set up and had a sound check. Des said he'd stay with the gear while we went out and got something to eat.

As we went into the town the Mods and Rockers were still baiting each other. The police presence told you that they were anticipating trouble later.

We had sausage and chips and a Tizer and then made our way back to the hall. A few people were drifting in, but it didn't seem to be getting full. This was unusual as we found that in places like this it was normally packed out. Perhaps one of the top bands was playing nearby. Tony said, with a laugh:

'They've probably heard about us and given it a miss.'

A bunch of girls came over to us for a chat while we were making the last checks. I've never seen girls so pleased to see us. I got chatting to a girl called Jackie, very petite with a bouffant hairstyle that made her look taller than she was. We hit it off straight away especially as she was wearing Chantilly perfume, third on my all-time list of favourites. She was nice, not loud or over the top. Jackie was somebody who you could take home to mum for afternoon tea. We got chatting as you do and she said:

'We girls are really pleased you're playing here tonight.'

'We're pleased to be playing here and the bonus is I've met you.'

I'm thinking I'm being clever with the old chat-up lines when she said:

'The problem is that none of the local bands want to play here.'

'Why's that, then?'

'They call this place Dodge City.'

It took a minute for the penny to drop.

'Jackie do I put two and two together and come up with the western about the Gunfight at Dodge City.'

'Yeah, not guns but everything else I'm afraid. It's got a terrible reputation for trouble. There's normally a fight every time there's a dance.'

'You're joking? I'll be back in a minute.'

The others had heard the bad news from the other girls. We needed to talk; we went into the kitchen, home from home to a family of rats. Should we do a runner or stay? Our brain said run, but our pride said stay. We minimised the equipment we were going to use in case there was any trouble. The newer amps and speakers went back into the van. There was a PA system of sorts which we could wire up. The sound wouldn't be that good but tonight was one of those nights when our equipment took priority. I used an old back-up guitar which was a Les Paul copy and the Fender went back in the case. Steve did the same with his bass. Des was going to stay with the van and park it down a side street while we were playing, to make sure it didn't get vandalised.

There was no stage; you played on the dance floor in front of the dancers, so no protection there. We felt like we were getting ready to go into battle, which was crazy. All we wanted to do was play music. A few bouncers came in with broken noses and biceps bulging. The bloke who was running it was a tosser; he didn't talk or take any interest in us whatsoever. All he was worried about was taking the five bob off the punters.

Jackie and her friends came over to us before the start and said they were looking forward to hearing us play. Jackie even gave me a peck on the cheek and said:

'Perhaps we can meet later for a coffee.'

❧ ❧ ❧

The room had now filled up, mostly with Mods. So we made sure there was plenty of what they wanted to hear. The girls we'd met were dancing in front of us which was good for the ego. Things were going well and we felt relaxed and it showed in our playing.

The first set finished with 'March Of The Mods' which got everybody up on the floor. Ray was really coming into his own fronting the band and tonight he'd come of age. We knew we'd picked the right guy. Steve was happy as he'd spoken to Jenny and she was coming to our gig in Bournemouth in a few days' time.

A few weeks ago Tony had stated that he was now going through a bohemian moment in his life and was at peace with the world. We took no notice of him as when he'd said it he'd had a skin-full of Double Diamond and was taking a few pills. It was noticeable his hair was getting much longer, in fact it was resting on his shoulders; he was also now sporting a droopy moustache. I looked over to him and laughed, he looked like Guy Fawkes, so much for us being a Mod band.

It was still going well as we started the second set. Then half way through it there was a right rumpus at the door.

You've heard of the Battle of Hastings in 1066 between the Norman and English armies. Well this was going to be the feckin' Battle of Hastings 1967-style with Mods and Rockers. These Rockers came storming in and it all kicked off. We stopped playing and tried to gather up our gear, no chance. A few of the Rockers headed our way intent in giving us a good hiding. Ray was a star and head-butted the first Rocker who came up to us. Then he goes into a boxing stance and starts laying into them. Steve and Tony are giving them as good as they get. Two of the Rockers jumped on me and I fought back but got a bloody nose for my trouble.

There were fights kicking off all over the dance floor as they knocked shit out of each other. Girls were screaming and running in all directions to escape the mayhem. Windows were getting smashed and so was our gear. Tony went haywire when this Rocker started kicking his drum set in. He got hold of him and laid him out with a couple of punches.

Suddenly it all stopped, people were disappearing out of windows and doors as the police arrived in force.

❧ ❧ ❧

I never did see Jackie as we left Hastings that night. We weren't going to hang about. We kipped in the van just outside the town; all of us had cuts and bruises. Tony's drum kit was a write-off and there was a lot of damage to two speakers, an amp and a mic. Fortunately the two guitars were still working, but had a bit of damage to the outside of them.

Des was gutted he couldn't help us, because he was riding shotgun in the van. We were pleased; if they'd got hold of our decent gear the tour would've probably been cancelled. Good job we'd kept the insurance payments up, at least we could put a claim in. We'd learnt our lesson way back when a similar thing happened at a New Year's party at Barking.

We found out why Ray was a bit tasty with his fists. He'd belonged to a boxing club and had had a few fights and was well on the way to appearing in the ABA championship when he decided on a musical career.

The only problem with this Sunshine Tour was that we were travelling all over the place doing these gigs, sometimes doubling back on ourselves – we were now off to Southend. We did have a word with Anthony before we left. He made it crystal clear:

'Do you want the work or not?'

❧ ❧ ❧

It wasn't only the drum kit we had a problem with. A couple of our speakers and an amp were now kaput after Hastings and we had to get replacements quickly before the next gig. Terry, a good mate of ours, played in a band called Terry and the Tanks. What a name for a band – we regularly took the piss out of the boys when we saw them. The band's name came from Terry's surname, Sherman; you couldn't make it up could you?

He was going to lend us what we needed. His band was playing up north, but his mum in Romford had a spare key to his place. His band rented a house out in Hornchurch and they always had a lot of gear as his dad had a music shop in Barking.

We picked the key up on the way back from Hastings and went to his house. It was early morning and still dark. The four of us went into the house and found the two Vox 30s and a Wem bass amp. It was like an Aladdin's cave of music gear and we had a good look around.

As we were taking the speakers and amp out of the front door it was like a scene from *Z Cars*. Suddenly there were police cars and a dog van outside the house and coppers jumping all over us. This hairy copper shouted out:

'You're nicked, lads, and you're coming down the station with us.'

We couldn't get a word in edgeways. Then the police dog comes out of the van and snarls in front of us. Steve shouts out:

'It's Sampson, Big Al's dog.'

The dog had gone from trying to bite us to jumping up and making a fuss after recognising us. His handler couldn't believe it.

'His name is Rusty, and he should be growling at you not giving you kisses.'

'I think he needs to be retrained, mate. He's just a softy at heart,' said Steve taking the piss.

We didn't let on about Sampson even though his handler kept asking us questions.

We were all handcuffed and taken down the nick. A neighbour thought we were breaking in and had phoned the police. Once they had spoken to Terry's mum we were released and sent on our way.

What an early morning call that was!

———————•———————

18

Back on the Road

Before the Southend show we stopped off at Tony's for a spare drum kit and full English, courtesy of his mum, which we needed after the fiasco around Terry's house. She didn't rate her son's new bohemian look and when we left she said:

'Go out the back door, Tony, I don't want the neighbours to see you like this.'

We stopped off at Rick's, he was well pleased to see us and said he was missing band life and being on the road.

Des was staying in Romford for a week, but said he'd join up with us later on in the tour. He had a bit of business to do regarding his greenhouse which had now multiplied to four.

Of course I went and saw my mum and she was well on the road to recovery. She wasn't impressed with the sticking plasters and bruises all over me. She commented that Arthur was being very helpful to her which was pleasing. The clump I gave him must've had some affect. Dad's visits down the Legion were now only four days a week, another result.

What was a surprise was that Anita had phoned my mum to see how she was and had sent her a bouquet of flowers. Straight away I said to mum:

'Did she ask about me?'

'Not really, she knew you were on tour and we just had a nice chat. She sounds a lovely girl. It's a pity your wayward ways can't stop, you could settle down with a nice girl like that.'

🐦 🐦 🐦

We did the Southend venue and I have to say I've never witnessed anything like it before in my life.

There were about 200 people in the large church hall. It was supposed to be booze-free, but everybody was bringing in Corona bottles filled up with alcohol, including us. The audience was mostly young people that had come to the dance but there were a few oldies, which was unusual. There was no stage, again we just played in front of the dance floor, which is fine if there's no trouble. We'd had one or two punch-ups in Southend before but hopefully with the vicar wandering about it would be a peaceful night.

The first set was a winner and the light ale in the Corona bottles was hitting the spot. We were about a third of the way through the second set when about eight people got up from the table they were sitting at and got on the dance floor. They were in their mid forties and had left a woman sitting in a wheelchair by the table. They'd definitely had too much pop as their dancing was well over the top, so much so that a lot of the other dancers got off the floor to watch and take the piss out of them.

We were enjoying their antics so we made 'Twist And Shout' last another five minutes, a wrong move. Suddenly one of the women who was dancing went over to the table, grabbed the wheelchair and started madly pushing it around. They were both pissed and the lady in the wheelchair was having a great time as her head bobbed up and down to the music.

The group of dancers decided to swing the wheelchair around. They pushed it to each other across the floor. The lady in the chair was going backwards and forwards and enjoying every minute of it. They were now clearly out of control and I looked at Tony, Steve and Ray to say lets finish the number. As I was playing the last chord, I looked up and saw this feckin' wheelchair flying towards us at speed. You know when something is going to happen and you can't do anything about it, this was it. They'd pushed it so hard that the bloke who was supposed to grab it missed his footing and fell over; it was now speeding in our direction. Steve, Ray and I jumped out of the way. Tony was stuck behind his drum kit so he couldn't get away and the wheelchair hit his drums full on. Fortunately the lady stayed in it and didn't get hurt; mind you she was well tanked up and just kept laughing at him. Tony went off his head after seeing his second drum set ruined. We had to hold him back as he was going to punch the lights out of the bloke who'd slipped and let the wheelchair go.

Afterwards we were supposed to go straight to Lyme Regis for our next gig, but had to stop at Tony's house to borrow another drum kit from his sister Penny, a brilliant little drummer; she had played with the band for a month when Tony had to have his appendix out. Absolutely knackered, we crashed out on the floor of Tony's house.

❧ ❧ ❧

We left early the following morning for Lyme Regis. Tony still had a cob on big-time and was swearing under his breath all the way there. You couldn't blame him, he had one drum kit destroyed by Rockers and another by a half-pissed wheelchair user. It didn't help when Steve said:

'Tony what happened to your peace with the world?'

'Get lost.'

We did the Lyme Regis show without incident and after the show we went to a party on the beach during which we indulged ourselves to the full.

The next morning, with splitting headaches, we headed for our next venue, a Weymouth holiday camp for two nights. Well I've never seen so many girls in one place. It was heaving, all trying to outdo each other with who could wear the least clothes. Because Steve was seeing Jenny in a couple of days, he decided to stay celibate.

We were shown the venue, we thought it was a just a hall but it was a theatre-cum cinema where everybody sat down to watch us. This was a different ball game. We soon sobered up and within an hour were rehearsing. As I've mentioned before when you've got hundreds of eyes looking at you, you don't want to make any mistakes. It was a top-notch theatre with a good size stage, and the real bonus for us was that they had all the amplification we needed including Marshall amps which were now the leading kit. Tony had a smile back on his face when he saw the Ludwig drum kit that meant he wasn't going for the three-card trick with drum sets.

Our chalet certainly wasn't glamorous; they put us together in a room with four bunks. After the *Tirpitz* experience with Steve I was going to have to try and find alternative sleeping arrangements.

It was a great night and we really enjoyed the gig. As soon as we finished we went to the Britannia, a large bar with a dance floor. The resident band was knocking out a Beatles number while we were enjoying a light and bitter and one of Tony's Golden Virginia roll-ups.

Next thing we knew Ray was on the dance floor giving it the twist, what a mover, he could certainly get around a dance floor. We nicknamed him the Top Twister after that. Everybody was looking at him and the girls were queuing up to dance with him. He came back to us for a slurp and was soon back on the floor again. He called Steve over to join him as he had two birds and wanted to break them up. Steve declined as he'd promised himself he would stay faithful to Jenny. That'll last about five minutes knowing him. I jumped in as substitute and ended up with a bird called Pearl, a precious jewel or one of unmatched beauty. She wasn't either of them, but she did have a low-cut top, short skirt and a nice pair of Bristols. After the twist we took them back to their table and bought them a drink.

The two girls, Gail and Pearl and another friend Iris, were from Rochdale and worked in a cotton mill. They were 18 and on holiday for a couple of weeks. They recognised us as two of the band that they'd just seen play. They were well chatty and hopefully up for it. We couldn't understand their lingo but that didn't matter as long as they knew the S word.

We're having a right laugh with the girls, unlike Steve. He was sat on his own drinking his pint of Red Barrel and smoking his rollup. Ray shouted over to him and wound him right up:

'Steve, they've got a mate called Iris, she's the one over there with the moustache and national health glasses.'

'I wouldn't take the piss, Ray, you're still on trial with the band.'

As we were winding Steve up, the bohemian floated into view. Tony had pulled this bird which he must've found in a witch's coven, she was scary. He acknowledged us and drifted away with her in a cloud of wacky backy.

ə❧ ə❧ ə❧

It was now getting near bedtime and we were looking to rearrange our sleeping arrangements. Without any persuasion Gail said:

'Do you want to come back to our place for a nightcap?'

Ray and I couldn't get the yes word out quick enough.

We followed the girls to their chalet or so we thought. We passed the chalets and were on open ground where there were loads of tents pitched. The girls suddenly stopped in front of one of these. We couldn't believe it when they went in; Ray and I were about to do a runner. They could see we weren't impressed with their accommodation and Pearl said sadly:

'We're only factory girls, we can't afford anything more than this.'

We weren't here for the decor so we bedded down for the night. Pearl had the decorators in, but she said she should be okay for tomorrow night, which was something to look forward to. We had a night of fumbling unlike Ray, he was an animal at it non-stop all night with Gail who seemed to be enjoying it. Mind you, there were a couple of problems, both noise-related. Ray, unbeknown to me, suffered from hay fever and all night he was sneezing and sniffling whilst he was banging away. The other irritant was an earth-moving shuffling noise which went on all night. We did try and find out what was causing it but without success.

ਦਾ ਦਾ ਦਾ

We met Tony and Steve for breakfast. Steve had the arse ache; he was finding celibacy, even for one night hard to take. With Ray and Tony going through detail by detail about their sexual conquests this certainly didn't help.

While Ray went to get another full English Steve and I had a quiet word with Tony about how much puff he was smoking. We'd also found a few pills in the chalet which weren't ours. He said it was none of our business and went off in a huff. As a close mate we didn't want him to become a Rock 'n' Roll statistic and six foot under.

We met Pearl and Gail on the beach later in the day. They brought along their mate Iris who was well rough. Steve, Tony and his girl Dawn joined us and as it happened we had a great day on the beach.

Later on in the day Steve and I hired one of those four-wheeled, two handle-bar, fun bikes from the camp. We pedalled around like maniacs, running everybody down. It had to end in tears when we lost control and ended up in the boating lake. We were soaked through and the bike was all bent up owing to the fact we hit one of the boats full on.

It was an okay gig in the evening. We'd played better but I think with a promise at the end of the night we'd other things on our mind.

It was straight from the stage to the tent for our night of lust with Gail and Pearl. Steve had sulked off somewhere, while Tony went back to Dawn's coven and probably more weed and pills.

Ray and I were having a good night with the girls, they certainly were very energetic but there was still this shuffling noise that seemed to be coming from under the airbed I was sharing with Pearl.

In the middle of the night a familiar voice from outside the tent whispered:

'Nick, Ray have you got a torch?'

'Christ Steve,' I replied, 'It's two in the morning, what do want a feckin' torch for?'

'I've lost it.'

'Lost what Steve?' I asked.

'You know.'

'For bleedin' hells sake, what have you lost?'

'My Durex.'

Ray and I put two and two together and came up with Iris who had the tent next to her mates.

'Hang about, Steve, you're not giving Iris one are you? Do you want a sack as well?' said Ray laughing his head off.

'Oh piss off, Ray.'

'What about Jenny? You're seeing her tomorrow. She won't be happy with you making Iris's dream come true,' I said.

'Look, have you got a torch or not?'

I put my head outside the tent, gave him a Johnnie and said:

'Be careful when you give her a snog; you don't want to get a burn mark from her moustache.'

He grabbed the French letter and pushed me back into the tent.

About an hour later there was this feckin' loud bang and the airbed I was laying on exploded. Pearl shouted out:

'Christ what's that?'

She grabbed a torch and let out a piercing scream as she shone it on an animal that had popped its head out of the deflated airbed. Gail saw the animal in the torch light and shrieked:

'It's a horrible brown thing and it's looking at me.'

With that, the two girls went loopy loo and rushed screaming out of the tent while we tried to catch the mole.

~ ~ ~

As we travelled to Bournemouth for the next show we were having a laugh about the mole. Steve took some stick about Iris, while Tony was in the back of the van zonked out from cannabis poisoning.

The Bournemouth gig was a nice touch. It was a theatre by the seafront and a good earner. That was the good news, unfortunately because it was high summer we couldn't get any digs for the night at a price we could afford, so it was going to be a choice between a kip in the van or on the beach.

Steve had scrubbed up well for Jenny; we dropped him off at the pier where he was going to meet her. I have to say I was well jealous, as I would've loved to have been meeting Anita. We agreed to meet him back at the theatre at 3.00 for some rehearsals.

We arrived at the theatre and unloaded the van. Well, only Ray and I unloaded it as Tony was still out of it. Tony's drug-taking was now getting to be a major problem. It was having an effect on his performance and that was no good for the band or him.

ঌ ঌ ঌ

Our agent Anthony had some really great news. It appeared our record had made the top ten in Holland and the promoters wanted us over there. With this in mind he'd booked us a one-off gig in Amsterdam as a starter. Even though it was just the one show, the money was excellent and a good leg-up for the band.

Steve turned up with Jenny wearing a big smile on his face, she did look pretty. We got stuck into the rehearsal and completed the final sound check.

It was a good dressing room and there was plenty of food on offer. Tony had come to and was hopefully listening to our advice about drugs. During a quiet moment Jenny came over and had a chat with me.

'How's your mum?'

'A lot better, thanks.'

'Anita sends her love to you Nick.'

'I wish she really meant it, Jenny.'

'In her own way she does. She still cares about you.'

'Will you thank her for phoning my mum and sending the flowers, that was really thoughtful of her?'

'Yeah, of course I will, Nick.'

The buzzer went and we made our way onto the stage. What a reception we got from the capacity audience. It was the first time I'd seen Ray look nervous. After a few numbers they were out of their seats and dancing in the aisles. We were on a roll; I don't think we'd ever played any better.

We finished the first set and went back to the dressing room for our twenty-minute break. We knew we'd played well – there's a real buzz when you know you're on top of your game.

After the gig Steve went back to Jenny's hotel room and we went on to a club. After kicking-out time we went and slept on the beach. I woke up with a girl from Swansea who as it happened was a fair piece; she paid for breakfast as well.

Gigs followed on the Isle of Wight, and at Hayling Island, Bognor Regis, Worthing, Dover and Herne Bay, then back to Essex where we did Canvey Island, Jaywick and Maldon. We gave ourselves a few days' break before heading south-west for the next part of the Sunshine Tour.

19

The Dream's Back On

I was glad to be home to see mum and have a rest before the next part of the tour. Steve was loved up with Jenny and was staying with her. We were going to pick him up on the way to Weston-super-Mare, our first night. Ray went back home to Barnet, and Tony, hopefully, was having a good rest and a drug-free few days.

Before we went our separate ways we met up with Tom; thanks to him the band's paperwork and advance bookings were in place. He'd brought some order to the band which is what we needed.

My mum thankfully was getting stronger and had some colour back in her cheeks. Without her jobs she was worried there wasn't enough money coming in. I soon put that right. With regular money now coming in for me I was able to give her some extra cash to ease her fears. My wanker of a brother was now actually pulling his weight helping mum while I was away so that was a plus. Dad had excelled himself and was now only going three nights a week down the Legion.

I'd arranged to meet Penny, Tony's sister; she was 18 and a really sensible girl. Before I went, I made my mum a cup of Camp coffee and left her listening to *Woman's Hour* on her Bakelite KB wireless, which looked like a toaster. Her sister Kitty was coming round so that was okay; I didn't like leaving her on her own.

I met Penny at Moka-Ris coffee bar in Elm Park and got straight to the point. The band was worried about Tony's drug taking – he was very close to his sister and he might listen to her. Penny was shocked and upset with the revelations and promised she'd have a strong word with him but wouldn't say that she'd met me. As previously mentioned before, Penny, like her brother, was an ace drummer and she and three other girls had just started up a band and had bookings already. In fact later we found out that her band was one of the first girl groups in Essex to be formed at that time.

We had another frothy coffee and a few laughs and she said she would keep in touch about Tony. I had to control myself as Penny was now looking a right little darling and didn't have a boyfriend. She must've seen it in my eyes when she said with a grin:

'Don't ask, Nick, as I might say yes and that could ruin a nice friendship.'

My next stop was Des; I found him under a Ford Zephyr at his lock-up. After the niceties I said to him in no uncertain terms:

'Des, I don't want you feeding any drugs to Tony.'

'I only do a bit of weed, Nick, I don't do pills.'

'Watch my lips, Des. You don't even give him a fag, get it?'

'Yeah, understood, does that mean I can't come on the south-west tour with you then?'

'Of course not, we'd love you to come, Des, but only if you take heed of what I'm saying.'

'It's registered, Nick.'

'Great, now my Cortina has a blow on the exhaust, can I leave it with you while I go into Harry Fenton's and get some new clobber?'

'No problem.'

I picked the motor up later and drove over to see Rick; he was well pleased to see me. The band missed him and so did the girls, although their fathers probably didn't! Rick said:

'The bottom line, Nick, is dad's been told by his brief that there is so much evidence against him, that if he puts in a plea of guilty he might get a lesser sentence for saving the court's time. But he will definitely get put away, that's for sure. Mum can't cope with the transport business, even with my help, so after the trial the business is up for sale.'

I didn't talk about the money his dad owed us; Rick didn't need that on top of him at the moment. He continued:

'How's my stand-in?'

'Yeah, Ray's fine, doing a good job.'

'Not too good I hope? I want to get back with the band as soon as possible.'

As I left Rick's I didn't have the heart to tell him Ray was great and it would be hard for him to get back.

❧ ❧ ❧

T.J. had rung while I was out so when I got home I rang him back; it was really good news. He'd met a guy in the bar of the hotel complex. He got talking to him and it turned out he was an executive with a record company. He told him about us and he offered to come and see us play.

He'd found out from our agent that we were on the Sunshine Tour in the south-west and had a couple of days off between gigs. He was going to book us on one of those days and the record company guy had agreed to come to the gig to hear us play.

It was double-bubble all round. I couldn't thank him enough. After the call I rang Tony and Ray – they were well chuffed. I then rang Tom to let him know about the extra booking and asked him to let Steve know when he rang home.

Steve belled me later, he was well happy about the record guy and the extra date at Reading.

With good news like this I needed to celebrate and have a laugh, but who should I celebrate with? Mandy came to mind, I hadn't spoken to her since her party, when she'd had a punch-up with her mum. I gave her a bell and as soon as she heard my voice she said in her strong Essex accent:

'Faaackinell, Nick, I didn't think you'd ring me again after the aggro at the party.'

She'd somebody else in tow, but she was up for seeing me, so it was a date. I picked her up later and we went to the Keys Hall in Dagenham and Mandy being Mandy, it was all on show and hanging out. The band playing that night was Johnny B and The Buzzards. It made a change to watch another group play, they weren't a bad band and it was a good night.

On the way home Mandy was very generous in the back of the motor and it certainly rattled the springs of the old Cortina, that was for sure.

᠃᠃ ᠃᠃ ᠃᠃

After a couple of days at home we were on our way to pick up Steve at Reading. Tony was a bit quiet in the back of the van, but certainly didn't look spaced out. Perhaps Penny had had a word with him. Ray was full of it and we had to listen about this bird he'd met at the Tottenham Royal.

When we arrived at Jenny and Anita's salon I was gobsmacked, this wasn't a tuppenny-ha'penny place. As I went in Steve was sat in a chair like King Canute having his hair cut by Jenny. There were another four stylists and some juniors, all busy with clients. They eyeballed me as I walked in. Anita wasn't there. The big gob then shouted out:

'This is Nick, the lead guitarist in my band.'

I nearly bit but I let him have his moment of glory. Jenny called out to one of the juniors to get me a coffee. Three of the stylists were girls and were all smiles. They all got smiles back especially one of them, she was gorgeous. About 20, with black hair cut in a bob, her makeup was immaculate and with her red top and matching skirt she was a cut above the rest. She'd just finished with her client and came over to me for a chat.

'All the girls in the salon are coming to the Embassy to watch you play. Steve's told us all about it.'

'I'll look forward to that. What's your name?'

'Shelly. I know your name, Steve told me.'

'Have you got any boyfriends on the go?'

She pouted her lips and said:

'Nobody loves me, Nick.'

Under my breath I said, 'I bleedin' do.'

'Perhaps we can meet up after the gig, Shelly?'

'That would be nice, Nick.'

Just then the front door opened and Anita was standing there. She didn't look too happy as she glared at Shelly:

'Haven't you got anything to do?'

Shelly moved away from me quickly and went to the back of the shop, visibly upset.

All the other staff kept their heads down as Anita went over to Jenny and said with a cutting edge:

'Mrs Cuthbert-Brown will be here in a minute and you know what she's like,' as she looked at me and Steve.

'I've finished Steve's hair and they're going now,' Jenny said.

'Don't worry, Anita,' I said, 'You haven't got to say hello and we don't want to lower the tone of the place for Mrs stuck-up Cuthbert-Brown, so we're off.'

I went over to Shelly to say goodbye and to get her phone number. Steve kissed Jenny and said he'd ring her later.

ॐ ॐ ॐ

As we made our way to Weston I couldn't believe what had just happened in the salon. Anita had blanked us just because we'd jeans and tee-shirts on. That wasn't the Anita I knew. Then Steve said with a swagger:

'Jenny and I are getting engaged, and getting married next year.'

There was total silence and then Steve said again:

'Aren't you pleased for us, then?'

'Just confirm to me, Steve, that means that you're off limits to any other girls.'

Steve stuttered and said:

'Well of course, Nick, I'm in love.'

Tony, Ray and me burst out laughing and took the right piss out him.

ॐ ॐ ॐ

The Weston gig was another two days at a holiday camp. We were playing one night in the bar and the other night in their dance hall. The entertainment manager was a bit arty farty, a guy in his thirties and a real fanny, it didn't help that he was a Jock, so you couldn't understand him either.

The first night was a calamity. It was in the Beachcomber Bar, which had just been refurbished. We had to dress up in Hawaii-type, colourful shirts and looked right knob-heads. The only plus was that the barmaids wore these grass skirts and if you looked hard enough you could see their knickers.

We were playing on a slightly raised, wooden platform. Behind the platform was a mural depicting a tropical island. It had a row of lights above it making it even more prominent. The mural ran the length of the bar and had only been put up the day before and was the brainchild of the Jock. He even had the local papers taking photos of him in front of it.

About an hour before we started playing Tony decided that a couple of the lights above the mural were shining in his eyes so they had to be adjusted. He found a ladder and a screwdriver and climbed up to adjust the lights. Suddenly the ladder wobbled and Tony fell off it and landed in a heap on the floor. In doing so the screwdriver caught the mural and gouged out a large chunk of it. The Jock, seeing his beloved mural with lumps out of it, completely lost it. He chased Tony out of the bar with the screwdriver in his hand shouting that he was going to kill him.

The next night we played in the dance hall. That wasn't much better as Ray had shagged the camp manager's daughter and got caught in the act. We wouldn't be getting an invite back there, that was for sure.

❧ ❧ ❧

Next stop Budleigh Salterton in Devon to play the Plaza. Before we left Weston I phoned Shelly. We were playing at Reading soon and hopefully this record guy was coming to hear us play, so I wanted to make sure I could see her after the gig. She seemed well chatty and I said:

'After the gig do you fancy meeting up?'

It all went quiet until she replied:

'I've been warned off you, Nick.'

'What are you talking about, warned off?'

'Anita told me that you were off limits.'

'You're having a laugh.'

'I wish it was because I'd love to see you again, Nick, but I value my job too much, sorry.'

'Is she still engaged to that plank, Simon?'

'Yeah, he's in the salon most days and they seem to get on fine.'

'So why has she put the block on you seeing me?'

'I don't know, look I've got to go, I'm still coming to the gig though, see you Nick, take care.'

The phone went dead; I tried to get hold of Anita at the salon to give her a volley. But the salon must have been closed for the day as I couldn't get any answer. Women, I'll never understand them.

༝ ༝ ༝

The Plaza sounded grand but it was another fleapit of a place. We humped the gear in and started setting up. We weren't very happy as it was a 9.00 to 2.00 in the morning gig. Five hours of playing with a few short breaks in between. It's nights like this when you feel like a travelling jukebox. It was fortunate that we had a full locker of songs. Long gigs like this were unusual. Being a holiday resort in the height of summer I suppose it made sense to the promoter. We did have the next day off so that was a bonus.

There was no dressing room; you got changed behind a grubby curtain full of holes. I thought Rick was a randy git but Ray was like a kid in a sweetshop. If it moved he shagged it. Tony was still puffing and popping, a bit of a worry as his drumming was starting to go downhill again. Steve was phoning Jenny three times a day and was loved-up big time.

I persuaded him to ask Jenny why Anita was so arsey in the shop. Being Steve he forgot, he was more concerned about how many times Jenny had told him she loved him. It was getting pathetic, but with so much talent on offer tonight, would he succumb?

We started the first set with an old favourite 'Twist And Shout' by Brian Poole and the Tremeloes. The twist was my favourite dance in the sixties. There were loads of others: The Turkey Trot, Penguin, Jive, Hitch-Hiker, Frug, The Shake, Jerk, Fly and the Locomotion. With five hours to play we would cover them all.

We were on top form, we really tore it apart. The riffs were fast and furious and we were sweating our bollocks off but enjoying every minute of it.

During a short break we were on the way to the bar when two right little darlings, each carrying the record sleeve of 'Suburban Mod' for us to sign, came over and started chatting. Both had dark hair, short skirts, tight tops, big smiles – right up our street. Ray had already eyed up a bird and was on the plot with her. Tony was more interested in a friend called hemp and had gone outside for a smoke. Steve succumbed to temptation immediately and we were now back as a double act. Ruth and Gillian were 19 and from a village called Littleham. Ruth means 'compassionate and beautiful', good enough for me!

We took them to the bar and ordered a couple of barley wines and we had a couple of pints of bitter from a local brewery, Norman and Pring. It had a bit of a kick to it so we had another couple before we went back on to play.

We saw the girls at each of the breaks and the vibes from them were red hot. Jenny was now a distant memory for Steve tonight as he and Gillian were all over each other. As we played the last number our thoughts were where are we going to take the girls at 2.00.

We packed the gear into the van. We hadn't got digs so it was going to be a van job, or so we thought, until Tony said he would be sleeping in it with a bird he'd pulled. In a way it was handy as we didn't want anybody tea-leafing the gear. Ray's luck was in, as his bird had a spare bed, actually just one bed. We arranged with Tony and Ray that we'd meet up at 11.00 the next day outside the Plaza.

Ruth and Gillian had told their parents that they were sleeping around each other's house in case they met someone. That was sound, but we had no digs to take them back to, so what to do?

I can confirm that the sand on the beach at Budleigh Salterton is very soft, but being woken up by the tide coming in and lapping round your arse isn't!

Later that day we met the girls again. Ruth's mother invited Steve, Gillian and me around for a meal. Homemade grub is not to be sneezed at when you're on the road so we were well up for it. After nicking some flowers from one of the garden beds along the prom we turned up. Her mum and dad were nice people and so was the steak and kidney pie, plum duff and cheese and crackers all washed down with real coffee, not that crap Camp my mum gives me.

We said we'd do the washing up while her mum and dad went into the other room to watch *Coronation Street*. You'd think after a whacking great tea and a night and morning of lust on the beach the four of us would've had enough. Wrong. As soon as they turned the television on we couldn't keep our hands off each other. While Elsie Tanner, Ena Sharples and Albert Tatlock were doing their thing on the screen we were doing our thing amongst the pots and pans.

The sound of the adverts had us in a panic and we'd just about got ourselves straight when Ruth's mum came in and says:

'How about a nice cup of tea, lads. I bet you could do with a break after all that washing up?'

How we kept it together when she said that I'll never know, especially as the washing up was still in the sink. We had our tea, she went back to *Coronation Street* and we had one for the road.

♪ 20 ♪

Could this be our Big Break?

From Budleigh Salterton we played Exmouth, Sidmouth, Dawlish and then across to North Devon at Barnstaple. From there it was back down to Reading for the gig, hopefully in front of the record guy coming to hear us play.

T.J. greeted us like long lost friends:

'Nice to have you back, lads. It'll be a big house tonight. I've plastered the town with posters and I've got rent-a-scream coming.'

He handed me a piece of paper.

'Here's a telegram from the guy from the record company confirming he's coming. I've given him the best room in the hotel; he'll be looked after like royalty.'

'We owe you T.J., you've been a diamond,' I said.

'Look, Nick, it's twofold. You're a class act, when you play here you put extra money on the gate. The kids in Reading love yer and tonight could be your lift off to stardom, so we all win.'

We were still having major problems with Tony. He was still popping and wasn't eating. He'd gone into his shell and was getting arsey about everything. At the last two gigs at Dawlish and Barnstaple his playing was a disaster, he was losing the plot so we had to have a word with him. Ray went to his room while Steve and I had a chat with him in the bar.

'Look, Tone, I've known you since we were kids ...'

'What's this, the Marjorie Proops hour, Nick? You two can get off my case.'

'Look we care about you, Tony. Whether you like it or not your drug taking is getting out of control and it's now affecting your drumming,' I replied.

Backing me up Steve said:

'Tonight is our big chance to get a record deal; a lot of people have gone to a lot of trouble to make this happen, we can't blow it.'

'Feck you two, I've had enough of you and the band so you can poke it up your arse and get yourself a new drummer, I'm off.'

And with that he kicked a chair over, smashed a glass against a wall and stormed out of the bar. T.J. was in the bar and came over:

'What's that all about, lads?'

'We've just lost our drummer. He's got the strops, he's well pissed off,' I said.

'Is he coming back, Nick?'

'Your guess is as good as mine.'

'Don't worry. In case he doesn't come back I can get in touch with our resident drummer, Lennie. He'll fill in for yer.'

'It ain't as easy as that.'

'Don't worry, he's mustard, he'll get you out of trouble. His band Lennie Harding and The Copycats have played the circuit for years and there's nothing he can't drum to. I'll bell him now; I know he's in because I spoke to him about an hour ago.'

As he left I thought to myself this is déjà vu. It was here that Rick left to go home when his dad got nicked – fortunately Ray helped us out. Then my mum got ill and I had to leave. Now we had Tony who's gone walkabout. When Ray joined us and we told him about Tony, he said:

'I'll give Billy a bell to see if he's available to finish the tour, if Tony doesn't show. Since Bad Brakes disbanded he's been working in a pub as a barman. I'm sure he'd jump at the chance to play.'

𝔞𝔞 𝔞𝔞 𝔞𝔞

It was all going tits up and we hoped Tony would get his brain back in gear and show his face. In the meantime we set the gear up on stage for the gig. About an hour later this bloke walks in and asked:

'Is Nick about?'

'That's me.'

'I'm Lennie. I gather you might need a drummer tonight?'

The three of us looked at him in amazement. He was about 40; his grey hair looked like it was plastered down with Brylcreem. He wore this tweed jacket and was wearing brown brogues. He'd have been more suited playing for the Billy Cotton Band Show, which my mum enjoyed on a Sunday afternoon. He could see we weren't impressed.

'Who'd you think was coming, feckin' Ringo Starr?'

We were lost for words.

'Do you want me or not?'

'Sorry mate,' I said, 'I suppose we were looking for somebody our age. If you can play drums and help us out tonight we'd be really grateful.'

'OK, give us the set list and we'll crack on. By the way,' he said with a laugh, 'It's about this time I have my Horlicks and rich tea biscuits.'

We all started laughing; at least he had a sense of humour. Lennie set the drum kit up and we had a quick run through. He was a helluva drummer; in fact he was probably the best drummer we'd heard in a long time. We concentrated on covers and just a couple of our own numbers.

We were of course hoping Tony would show his face, but the longer it went on the more worried we became.

We'd just stopped for a break and while Lennie was flashing the Craven A, a bloke of about 30, wearing a smart suit entered the hall and came over to us. He was stocky and had a crew-cut.

'Who's Nick,' he said with a cut-glass accent.

I muttered to myself, 'I'm popular today.'

'Why, who wants him?'

'That doesn't matter, are you him or not?' he said in an aggressive manner.

'Well as it happens I am, who wants him?'

He got right up close to my face and said;

'I'm Simon Chandler and I'm Anita's fiancé. I'll say this just once. Keep well away from her otherwise you'll come a cropper, do I make myself clear.'

'Who the bleedin' hell do you think you are?'

'I'm your worst enemy if you don't listen to what I'm saying.'

'Is that meant to scare me?'

'You might think you're some kind of rock star, but in my eyes you're nothing. I warn you, stay away.'

Ray moved in front of him and said:

'You have a go at him and you have a go at all of us.'

Feeling brave after Ray's comments I said:

'I'll tell you what, I thought Anita had class. You're just a Hooray Henry who's got a plum in his gob. You can get out of my face and go back to the office and play with your abacus!'

He looked at me and I thought he was going to bury me. He could've done as he was one big lump. He had a final look, uttered some more threats and left the hall.

'Thanks, Ray, that was top-class, mate, I didn't see you come forward, Steve.'

'He's a big'un, I value my good looks.'

Lennie added:

'He's the local celebrity around here. He's captain of the main rugby team in town and there's always pictures of him in the newspapers at charity events, etc. His parents own a lot of businesses around here. Simon Chandler is the original silver spoon boy.'

❧ ❧ ❧

It was now 5.00 and Tony still hadn't shown. It didn't look good as he'd taken all his clothes out of his room. The only good news was that Billy was available to finish the Sunshine Tour if needed and we could pick him up from the station tomorrow. The next night we were playing Paignton.

We were on at 8.00 so we went back to the hotel to freshen up and have some food. Steve was feeling guilty about meeting Jenny, after playing sandcastles with Gillian on the beach and the kitchen table. *Coronation Street* will never be the same after that.

We made our way to the hall and saw T.J. on the way wearing a Tonic suit, so shiny you needed sunglasses when you looked at him.

'Tony hasn't shown then, Nick?'

'No, he's dropped us right in it.'

I looked at Lennie and laughed:

'He's a great drummer but it's like playing with your dad.'

'I see you had a run in with golden bollocks Simon Chandler, then?'

'How'd you know that?'

'I know everything that happens in this town. Anyway I can't stop, the guy from the record company has just turned up and I'm going to wine and dine him.'

'It would be nice if we could meet him,' said Ray.

'All in good time, Ray.'

'You sound like our manager,' said Steve.

T.J. winked and said:

'You never know.'

After we had the last sound check there was a phone call. I rushed to pick the phone up in the foyer hoping it was Tony.

'Hiyah, Nick, it's Rick just ringing up to wish you and the boys the best of luck tonight, hope it goes well.'

'That's well decent of yer, mate. It's a pity you're not here with us.'

I told him about Tony, he wasn't surprised as he'd seen him with a local drug dealer in Romford before the Sunshine Tour. He had tried to warn him off the bloke but he was having none of it.

It was sad that Rick was no longer in the band and with Tony now on a slippery slope with drugs, it looked like his days with the band were numbered. Steve and I had known him since we were kids and he was the leader of the band when we first formed Tony and the Mustangs at 11 years of age. Recruiting Rick as our singer had been the icing on the cake. We'd had some great laughs together. Now the two of them were no longer with us and that was really sad.

I was still dreaming of the past when we heard the sound of giggling coming from outside the dressing room door. The door opened and all the girls from the salon plus a few more, led by Jenny, came bundling in, but no Anita. They must have had a contest to see who would wear the shortest miniskirt. Shelly was definitely the winner and I made my way over to her. Ray got among the other girls and Steve was down Jenny's throat in an instant. Lennie looked on in amazement as bedlam reigned and I said to Jenny with a giggle:

'Meet our new drummer Lennie, have any of the girls got a mum looking for a bit of action?'

I then edged over towards Shelly and said:

'Can't we have a meet after the gig?'

'I'd love to Nick, but it's Anita, you know what I mean.'

I told her about Simon coming on all heavy. She seemed shocked which put a different complexion on it.

'If Anita doesn't come tonight you've got yourself a date, Nick.'

There was so much noise and laughter we didn't hear the bell go for the start of the show. T.J. rushed in and said:

'Lads, you can have the ladies after the show, there's an audience and a record company waiting for yer. Get out there and do the business. The girls left and we picked up our guitars. We were just leaving when Lennie said:

'Guys it's your big moment, take a tip from an old pro. Impressing the punters is of course important, but its how you play tonight that will get you that record deal. Be professional, go out there and put on a show to be proud of.'

We thought that was a great shout from Lennie, we all hugged and wished each other luck. As we made our way to the stage the audience was screaming:

'Modern Edge, Modern Edge.'

It made your hair stand on end, as we came on stage; the decibels went up an octave. The atmosphere was nothing like I'd ever witnessed before. The lights suddenly lowered, the spotlights were on us. We waved to the crowd as we plugged in the guitars. I switched on my Copicat Watkins echo box to the backdrop of a stack of Marshall amps. Ray deliberately and slowly adjusted the Shure mic, nicknamed the skull head by bands because of its shape. The screaming was now deafening as Lennie drummed four beats to start the night off with 'Suburban Mod'.

Ray had them in the palm of his hand as he strutted around the stage song after song. We now felt like an established band and we deserved another chance at the elusive record deal. I looked across the stage to Steve as the bass notes were coming through fast and furious from his Hofner. His smile said it all as we finished the first set with a number we had written, a rock-type ballad with plenty of meaningful lyrics and a great guitar solo. We left the stage to a roar of approval from the capacity crowd.

We were sweating buckets and enjoying a beer in the dressing room when T.J. raced in full of enthusiasm. He was smoking a large Cuban cigar and holding a glassful of scotch and ice.

'Unbelievable lads, you were out of this world. The record guy is well impressed. If the second set is as good as the first you've got a great chance of cracking a deal. Steve laughed and said:

'T.J., this geezer ain't the invisible man is he?'

'He's real, don't worry about that.'

And with that he was out the door. Lennie came back in after having a leak, and Ray remarked,

'Lennie, your drumming was spot on, we owe you.'

Steve and I endorsed his comments, he'd been top drawer. At gigs like this we liked to change our tops after the first set. We went from target tee-shirts to white Ben Sherman half sleeve shirts. Lennie went from a Val Doonican jumper to a red blazer!

🐦 🐦 🐦

As we kicked off the second set the girls from the salon were right in front of us and were shouting and screaming. It came as a bit of a shock, when I saw Anita was amongst them and seemed to be enjoying herself.

We'd played here a few times but it was the first time that the crowd were bobbing to the music instead of dancing.

It was a crazy night and we filled our boots to the full, lapping up the adulation from the audience. If you could bottle this you'd make millions.

As we came towards the end of the second set the crowd surged forward and shouted for more, and they got it. We didn't bother with an encore or, as it's better known in the music industry, 'a false tab'; we just played. There had to be an end and we went out with 'Hi Ho Silver Lining' by Jeff Beck.

As we sat down in the dressing room, nothing was said for a minute or two, we were completely knackered. The silence was shattered when T.J. came bounding through the door, vaulted a couple of chairs like a Grand National winner and landed in front of us.

'That was ace lads. John H. Fitzgerald, the record company guy, wants to see you in my office at 10.00 sharp tomorrow.'

And with that he was out as quick as he came in. Within seconds he was back.

'Sorry, lads, the drinks are on me.'

With the promise of free drinks and four happy bunnies we went straight into the hotel bar. We felt like stars as we were mobbed by a load of girls. I made a beeline for Shelly, her smile said it all. Steve was all over Jenny, while Ray was chatting up another of the girls from the salon. Lennie was enjoying his moment of fame with a pint of Guinness and a cigar. He'd pulled an OAP, she was all over him!

I was just having a nice chat with Shelly when she suddenly pulled away from me and rushed off to the toilet. I knew the reason why, as coming towards me was Anita. On reaching me she said rather curtly:

'We need to talk.'

We went outside into the warmth of the night and sat down on a seat in the small hotel garden.

Before she said anything I thought I'd get in first.

'Anita, have I hassled you in the last few weeks?'

'Well, no.'

'Have I phoned you up and been nasty to you?'

'Of course you haven't, Nick.'

'So why did you make me feel like I'd trodden in something when you were going on about Mrs Cuthbert-Brown in your salon ...'

'But ...'

'No, you listen. I know I might not be the smartest dressed dude around town, and probably don't fit in with the salon's decor. But I don't expect you to stick your nose up in the air, because Mrs bleedin' Cuthbert-Brown is coming in for her rinse.'

'There's no need to swear, Nick.'

I was now on a roll and couldn't help myself.

'I play in a rock band so you have to take me as I am.'

'I do, Nick.'

'And while we're about it why did you warn Shelly off about seeing me, she's scared shitless of you. That's not the Anita I know, the one who rang my mum up when she was ill and sent her a bouquet of flowers.'

'Is there anything else you want to throw my way, Nick?'

'Yes there is. I don't need your so called fiancé Simon Chandler, who seems a right plum, coming up to me in front of my mates threatening to knock my lights out if I contact you.'

'What? I don't understand, Nick. I know nothing about this.'

'It's a wonder he's not chaperoning you tonight, protecting you from big bad Nick?'

'Have you finished because you're really upsetting me?'

I could tell from the tone of her voice and the tears in her eyes that I'd probably gone over the top.

'Nick, when I came into the salon that morning I was having a bad day. You have to remember when we first met four years ago we were just kids having fun without a care in the world. I now own a business with eight staff which brings its own pressures.'

'I understand, Anita.'

'With the greatest respect, I don't think you do, Nick. The Mrs Cuthbert-Browns of this world pay my wages. I wasn't being snobbish towards you; I think you know me better than that. When I saw you with Shelly I was out of order, I shouldn't have said that. If I'm honest I was jealous.'

'Anita ...'

'Let me finish. You can't come back into my life when you feel like it and expect everything to be the same.'

'What about when we went to Weston.'

'That was a mistake.'

'Well it didn't feel like it.'

'Well it was, Nick. With the kind of lifestyle you lead with your band you're in and out of people's lives every day. You go from one girl to another and I don't think you realise that people have feelings. It's not like a tap that you can turn on and off when you want to. And while we're about it, if you really think Jenny doesn't know what Steve gets up to when he's not with her then I'm afraid you must think we're really stupid. It was the same when I went out with you, you were no different. You might think Steve and you are some form of rock stars, and that you have the right to treat girls like pieces of meat.'

'Hang about, it's not like that at all, that's well out of order. We don't do anything that nobody wants us to do.'

'Let me finish. I'm truly sorry that Simon confronted you and said what he said. I told him about you when I first met him and knowing you were playing in town he put two and two together.'

'Is that it then, Anita?'

'I think it is, Nick.'

'Whatever you think about me, Anita, I still have feelings for you.'

'Don't go there, Nick.'

She got up and ran off crying.

&v &v &v

At 10.00 Steve, Ray and me were facing John H. Fitzgerald in T.J.'s. office. Here was a man of about 40, a smart dresser with an air of authority who spoke in a soft southern Irish accent. After the introductions he got straight to the point.

'You know my name and I represent a well-known record label. If you like, I'm their talent spotter and I have full responsibility for taking on new acts. You're not unknown to us as we had somebody look at you a while back when your last record company released you.'

We were surprised with his comments and we knew we weren't dealing with a dummy.

'I don't know whether it was a set-up last night by T.J. but the young people loved you. If it was a set-up, I'd get him to manage you,' he said with a laugh. 'A couple of your own numbers, especially with a stand-in drummer, were good, in fact very good. By the way where was your drummer last night?'

Quick as a flash Ray said:

'He had to go to his granddad's funeral.'

'I'm sorry about that.'

'Yeah, he was close to him, he taught him to play drums when he was a kid,' lied Ray.

There was a pregnant pause as he looked at us to see whether it was a load of bollocks we were spinning him. He didn't see a flicker from us so he continued:

'All these covers you're playing are not creating your own individual sound. You're in between a sort of Mod-Pop band and you need to find your own identity. Having a hit record with your own material is not easy unless you're McCartney or Lennon. But it doesn't mean we wouldn't use your material if we think it's good enough. We're good at what we do and we treat our artists right. We don't mess them about and we don't like being messed about. If you did come on board with us, you would do what we tell you, to the letter. The financial rewards could be huge, especially if it's your own songs. We have an office in America and we're well represented all over Europe.'

'Where do we sign, then?' said Steve with a big grin on his face.

'We're a long way from that, son. What I will say is that I think you've got what it takes to be a chart-topping band. But before any of that I want to see a copy of the contract you had with your previous record company to see whether there are any hidden clauses in it.'

Alarm bells were ringing as I said anxiously:

'But they got rid of us. I don't understand?'

'What I need you to do is to get your manager to send me a copy of the contract.'

He handed me his card; the company had an office in the West End of London.

'I'll be in touch as quickly as possible once we have looked at the contract.'

As he left the room, T.J. came in.

'How'd it go, lads?'

'Well if it all pans out we could have ourselves a record deal,' I said excitedly.

'That's a right result, lads, well done. After dealing with you boys and John H. Fitzgerald I'm thinking of starting up my own agency running bands, and you could be my first signing.'

'As it happens Fitzgerald said you'd make a great manager,' piped up Steve.

'There we are, lads, it could be a marriage made in heaven. Oh by the way I've had a word with your agent and booked you for a weekend in September.'

'That's fine, you know we like playing here,' I said.

♪ **21** ♪

———— ◆ ————

Back on the Sunshine Tour

While the lads went to pick up Billy from the station I had calls to make. Mum was first on the list, her voice sounded a lot stronger so that was good news. I knew she was feeling better when she bollocked me for not sending my prick of a brother a birthday card.

Next call was to Tom to get him to send a copy of the last contract to the new company. Fortunately he hadn't slung it in the bin. I told him about this new record guy and what he'd said. He was crystal clear; never sign anything without him being there. That of course went without saying. He'd been in close contact with our agent and even got bookings for 1968. I told him about Tony and suggested we pay him for another week or two to see whether he was coming back to the band.

I rang Penny and told her about her brother. She was devastated because she knew he was on a downward spiral with his drug taking. I told her that Tom had the phone numbers of our gigs on the Sunshine Tour if she wanted to contact us.

I got in touch with Rick who was pleased the gig went well with the record company. He hoped he would be rejoining the band pretty soon; that could be a problem as Ray was doing a fantastic job as our singer and we didn't want to lose him.

The last call was to Des to tell him about Tony in case he had heard from him. He took it bad as he felt that maybe some of his puff was to blame.

❧ ❧ ❧

As we made our way to Paignton with Billy on board we felt that it was starting to go our way. He was happy playing in a band again. He was a right piss taker and you had to be on your guard because you never knew what he was going to get up to. And you wouldn't pick a fight with him – he was barrel-chested with arms like logs. Ray said they'd called him Hercules at school.

When we stopped for some grub at a roadside cafe I had a quiet word with Steve:

'How did you get on with Jenny?'

'Well the engagement's off,' he said with a laugh. 'What about Anita, how did that go?'

'Not good. She gave me a real pasting about my lifestyle and how I treat girls. Do you know, she was right? She's probably the only girl that I've ever really cared about.'

'I had the same third degree from Jenny. They're a couple of really great girls who are going places with their hairdressing business.'

'Where's that put us, Steve?'

'Paignton, in about an hour, mate!'

ॐ ॐ ॐ

After the euphoria of Reading, Paignton was a bit of a come-down. The air-raid shelter that doubled as a dance hall was scruffy and uninviting.

As soon as we arrived we set the gear up as we needed as much practice as possible with Billy. We'd only heard him play for a couple of minutes when we were in Manchester. As we played 'With A Girl Like You' by The Troggs I thought feckin' World War Three had started; he was knocking shit out of the drum kit. I couldn't hear myself play. After a few bars I stopped playing and said to Billy:

'Your family in Barnet ain't Apaches are they?'

'What do you mean by that, Nick?'

'I thought you were sending feckin' messages back home to them on your drums.'

'Are you trying to say something?'

I looked over to Ray and said:

'Have a word with your man, he's giving me a right headache; I'm going for a smoke.'

Steve joined me outside for a drag and I said to him:

'We've been on the road for nearly four years, how many days have we had off in that time?'

'Not many, Nick.'

'You know, Steve, I feel knackered and when a set of drums are giving me a headache something's wrong?'

'I know what you mean. The thought of two weeks on the road with Billy doesn't bear thinking about. No wonder he ain't with another band.'

'And I still can't get Anita out of my mind, she's got to me. Everything she said about me was spot on. How have I let her slip through the net, Steve?'

Ray came outside and joined us.

'You've upset him now. He's threatening to come off the tour,' he said.

'Ray, I have to ask you, how did you work with him with that racket he makes, he could wake the dead.'

'Sorry, Nick, I didn't hear that. I've gone deaf!'

We pissed ourselves laughing and lit up another fag.

Billy did calm it down a bit, but if Tony wasn't coming back on board, he wasn't the long-term answer.

Of course we were waiting for that phone call from the record company to say we had a deal. Later on in the day the

girl in the office said that there was a call for me. It wasn't
the record guy but Penny. I couldn't believe what she told me.
After the call I said to the boys:

'You ain't going to believe this? Tony's just surfaced back at
Romford and listen to this, he's had enough of band life and
he's off to India to meditate and discover another world.'

'India, you're having a laugh,' said Steve.

'I kid you not, he's told Penny to tell us he's sorry he left
us in the lurch but wishes us the best of luck with the band.'

'He'll discover another world in India that's for sure. My
mate went over there and sat on the bog for a month,' laughed
Ray.

'She said he's gone all peaceful and has made up his mind
that's what he wants to do.'

After all the piss-taking, Steve, Ray and I had a chat. We
needed a drummer, pronto.

'Anyone know another drummer who can play and fit in
with us?' I asked.

'You don't fancy Billy, then,' said a grinning Ray.

'You are jesting, Ray?' replied Steve.

We did the show, but after the previous gig it was a damp
squid. Playing to about 80 people we just couldn't get it
together and we played crap. It was so bad we felt guilty about
taking the money.

ॐ ॐ ॐ

We were now on our way to the English Riviera for two
nights at the Wickham Hall in Torquay.

The first night in front of about 200 people was okay.
After the gig the other three went to a party. I wasn't in the
party mood after having had a bloke with a pneumatic drill

doubling up as our drummer behind me for three hours. I just wanted to be on my own and went into a local all-night coffee bar called Negresco.

I was having my frothy coffee and being an advert for Billy no mates, when three girls joined me at the table. One of them had a big gob on it, she just wouldn't stop talking. All I wanted was a bit of peace and quiet. One of the other girls looked at me and winked as if to say, yeah she has got a big mouth.

You know when you think it's best to keep your thoughts to yourself. Well I didn't. I raised my voice and said:

'Do you know, luv; you could get a job as bleedin' Torquay's town crier.'

If looks could kill I'd be dead. Now the whole of the room had come to a standstill and you could hear a pin drop.

'What did you say to me?'

'All I said was, it would be nice if you kept your voice down as you're giving me and probably everybody else a bleedin' migraine.'

Her mouth opened and shut about six times. She looked around the coffee bar and could see that she had no support. She got up and said with more venom than a rattlesnake:

'You're nothing more than a London lout who's got no respect for girls. I hate you.'

She picked up her coffee cup and threw the contents in my face. She got more pissed off when she realised it was empty and stormed out followed by one of the other girls. As she went out the crowd cheered. I felt really embarrassed as I knew I'd gone over the top and shouldn't have sworn at her. The other girl who was left at the table looked at me, grinned and said:

'I know hundreds of people who would've liked to have said that to her. She's a pain in the arse.'

'Sorry, I was really out of order; by the way what's your name?'

'Melanie, Mel for short.'

The manager carried two coffees over and put them on the table with a grin:

'I'd have loved to have done that, mate. She's always in here scaring the customers away, well done.'

Mel got up from the table and was about to leave.

'My last bus goes in about ten minutes.'

'That's a shame it would've been nice to have had a chat with you.'

She looked at me for a second or two and said:

'Yeah why not, I can get a taxi home.'

'Shouldn't you let your mum and dad know you'll be a bit late?'

'There's no need, I room with some other girls.'

My expression changed immediately and it was 'up periscope', but I was soon put in my place.

'I only have a single bed so drink your coffee because that's the only hot thing you're going to get tonight.'

I roared with laughter and she started giggling as well.

What a great sense of humour Mel had. She was 18, with long black hair and wore the fashion of the day, miniskirt, a white, short-sleeved shirt with a small, black, knotted tie. She shared a house with four other girls and was a shorthand typist in Torquay.

'Where've you been tonight?' I asked.

'Went to the pictures and saw *Billion Dollar Brain* with Michael Caine, not a bad film. But tomorrow's the night we're looking forward to.'

'Why's that? Well there's a band called Modern Edge playing at the Wickham Hall and I've heard they're really good.'

I'd normally have given it the big one about me being in the band. But it was just nice talking to a girl without showing off. We had our coffees and went and sat down by the seafront.

Have you ever met somebody who's a complete stranger and within an hour you end up telling each other your life story? Well tonight was that night. I didn't mention the band at all but all the other nitty gritty came out. We stopped talking about six in the morning. The sun was coming up as I walked her to the bus stop. She allowed me to kiss her and I said:

'Perhaps we can meet at the dance tonight?'

'I'm not sure, Nick, I'm going with some friends.'

'I'm going anyway. I'll be right down the front of the hall.'

'You never told me what you're doing down here, Nick?'

'Just a bit of this and that, maybe see you tonight, Mel.'

'Yeah, maybe, Nick.'

🐦 🐦 🐦

In the morning I was on the stage checking the gear when the other three came back from the party. They were well wrecked. Steve had fallen in love again, while Ray reckoned that Devon girls were definitely for him and he was going to move down here permanently. That would change when we played Cornwall. Billy had a first, and met a girl who liked his drumming, so he was happy.

Des rushed into town in his jeep with his latest flame. Looking at her, it wasn't good. He took the usual stick from us.

'Des it's nice to see you, mate,' said Steve, 'But why bring her, it's not Hallowe'en already is it?'

'Steve, now and again your jokes get a bit jaded. For your information she's a lovely girl with a heart of gold. Blanche and I are now a couple.'

'Blanche? How can you go out with a bird called that?'

Poor old Des, he does pick them.

'By the way, changing the subject, Des, have you seen Tony?' I asked.

'Yeah he's flipped and he's off to India next week with this bird he met, she's turned his head with all this meditation and inner body crap. And by the way, he wants his drum kit back when the tour finishes, he's sold it to a mate of his. He's given him the money up front, that's how he's getting part of his airfare.'

I looked over at the drum kit that now looked like it was ready for Steptoe's yard after Billy's handiwork.

Des was staying for tonight's gig and the one at Falmouth in a few days' time. The others had gone back to the digs for a kip so he was looking at the van because there was a knocking sound coming from the engine.

The receptionist let me make three phone calls. The first was to my mum, she was still improving health-wise. The only blip was Arthur, he'd got the sack from another job. Mum got a bit upset when I said perhaps he wasn't cut out for work! She told me that Anita had rung.

'She's such a nice girl, she asked me how I was and we had a lovely chat, she sounds a very caring person. You'd do well if you settled down with her, instead of chasing all these popsies around the country.'

'Okay, mum, point taken, so what did she want?'

'She's left me a number for you to ring her, and remember what I've said, she's a smashing girl.'

I was really surprised about the call, but there was no reply when I rang her.

The next call was to Tom. John H. Fitzgerald had phoned him to say thanks for the copy of the contract which his legal people would be looking at. He was going to America for a couple of weeks and he'd contact us as soon as he got back. He said if there were no glitches in the contract, he'd talk to us about a record deal. It doesn't get any better than that because they were a big outfit and well-known in the music industry.

I rushed to tell Steve and Ray who of course were delighted that we'd been given another chance. We had a Tom Thumb cigar and a cup of tea. We certainly knew how to celebrate!

The last call was to Rick:

'There's some good news and bad news', he said. 'Dad has been to court and because his brief says it was an open-and-shut case he pleaded guilty. He got three years which he thought was a result. Dad had already got a buyer for the business knowing he was going inside. That should be put to bed in the next few weeks, so I will be your singer again soon.'

My reply was not a bundle of joy as Ray was proving a great asset to the band. I couldn't see us getting rid of him for Rick. I waffled a bit and said I would see him when we got back.

I had a quick word with Steve and he agreed with me that we'd cross that bridge when we came to it. The only problem we had now was that Billy knew we needed a drummer and was putting his name in the frame.

❧ ❧ ❧

About an hour before the gig I tried Anita again. I'd rung a couple of times before so when she answered I was somewhat lost for words:

'Hi, hiyah, Anita, it's Nick, you rang me.'

'Nick, I'm glad you rang me back. First of all I'm really sorry I had a go at you, you were right about a lot of things you said about me.'

'It's me who should say sorry. I went a bit over the top, I really didn't mean it. I'll be totally honest, Anita, I still really like you, what more can I say?'

It all went quiet. I thought the phone had gone dead.

'You know I've still got feelings for you, Nick, and find it very hard to push you out of my life.'

'Anita, I'd better go because I'm being the old Nick again.'

There was a short laugh and Anita said:

'I think your mum is trying to marry us off.'

'I'm sorry about that, she does have a way with words.'

'She seems really nice; anyway I'd better go, too; best of luck with the tour.'

'Thanks, we're playing Reading again soon, it's like our second home. Perhaps we can have a drink together.'

'Perhaps, see you, Nick, take care.'

&❧ &❧ &❧

There's going to be an extra edge to our playing tonight after the great news about the possible record deal. As we're having a quick sound check a bunch of Irish teenagers come over and one of them asks:

'Could you play The Yenka tonight?'

For a minute I think he's called me a wanker.

'Sorry, mate, ain't got a clue what that is,' I say.

We later find out it's a dance record by an Irish show band called The Freshmen and is all the rage in Ireland.

We're ready to start the gig. There's a good crowd and we're up for the craic as the Irish would say. I look out for Mel but can't see her.

We start off with a bit of The Who, 'Pictures Of Lily', which normally gets them going. Then I see Mel right at the front of the hall, just a matter of feet from the stage. When she sees me she is flabbergasted. Once she gets over the shock there's a nice smile.

Later in the first set, when it's all going so well, I notice the gobby bird from the coffee bar on the dance floor. When she notices it's me on the stage her face turns to thunder. With her are a few blokes, a bit on the big side.

After the first set I jumped off the stage to see Mel.

'You're a dark horse, Nick; most blokes would've been full of themselves playing in a band.'

'Not me, Mel, I don't like showing off!'

I arrange to see her later. Then trouble looms – the gobby girl comes over to me with the three blokes. She points at me and says:

'That's him; he's the one who was rude to me.'

The biggest one steps forward and growls:

'No one's rude to my sister. We'll be waiting for yer after the dance, you grockle.'

He pushes me away and goes back to his sister and the other two blokes. I later find out that a grockle is a term used by Devonians for holidaymakers.

I get back on the stage; the other three have seen the confrontation and Billy asks:

'What was that all about, Nick?'

'Nothing mate, forget it.'

'There must've been something', Ray added.

'There was, but I don't want to offend you and Billy.'

'What's all that about not wanting to offend us?'

'Well, the bloke who pushed me, him and his mates saw us play a while back when Rick and Tony were in the band. They reckoned the new singer was tone deaf and useless.'

Looking at Billy I continued:

'They thought you were the worst drummer in the world. Well of course I was sticking up for you two when he pushed me away.'

Billy and Ray go off their heads and are about to jump off the stage and do 'em there and then. I pull them back but they're on fire and are going to have blood.

Just before we start the second set Steve whispers in my ear:

'What're you up to, Nick?

'Me, I don't know what you mean?'

The gig goes well and as we're loading the gear back in the van, the three blokes come around the corner and walk towards us. I shout over to Ray and Billy:

'Would you believe it, that's the three blokes who reckoned you two were crap.'

You have to remember that Ray is a top amateur boxer and Billy is one big lump, so they make a fearsome duo. Within two minutes it's all over. Ray has laid out the girl's brother with one punch, while Billy's done the same to another one. Billy then goes for the last one, puts him in a headlock and squeezes him so hard I think he's bleedin' croaked it. The three limp away, probably thinking to themselves that's the last time they'll pick a fight.

ैं ैं ैं

Next it was Plymouth which was all right until the Navy and Army decided to have a punch up on the dance floor. We abandoned ship and headed for Falmouth in Cornwall where we were meeting Des.

We met him and Blanche at the venue, a village hall in the backwater. Tonight was going to be a real wind-up. We hauled the fogger and wind machine out of the Transit along with the other gear and set up. We were going to dump them after the gig as they were taking up too much space in the van. But we were going to have some fun with them first.

Always in the back of our minds was that phone call from John, the record company guy, to confirm whether we had a deal. It hadn't happened yet, but hopefully we wouldn't have to wait too long.

We were now ready to party. The atmosphere was ace, and with the lights low all we could see was the heads staring towards us. What a great feeling as we started with '5-4-3-2-1' by Manfred Mann. The night got better and better – even Billy's drumming was improving. Ray was singing his heart out while Steve and I were just enjoying the moment.

It was now time for the fun to begin. Both the fogger and wind machine were plugged in. Des was in charge of these. Ray got on the mic and exhorted the crowd:

'Come on girls, get on the dance floor, the blokes can have a rest. It's a twist competition and the three best dancers will get a signed copy of our latest record. So come on, girls, get your twisting shoes on and show us how good you are.'

So far so good, as a load of girls got on the floor to dance. We went straight into 'Twist And Shout'; the girls were wiggling their arses, much to the delight of the band. We gave Des the nod and the old fogger went into action. There was now a light mist covering the dancers which hid our real intentions. We gave another nod to Des to switch the fogger off and switch the wind machine on.

It came on like a feckin' hurricane and had the desired effect in lifting up the girl's skirts. There was red, black, white, blue, flowered; it was like the shop floor at Marks and Spencer's knicker department. There were even some naughty ones who'd none on at all. The girls were trying to keep their skirts down while the industrial wind machine was on full blast. The girls were screaming while the blokes had their eyes popping out of their heads, what a great laugh.

The management didn't see the joke and gave us our marching orders, calling us bleedin' Emmets, Cornwall's equivalent to Devon's Grockles.

It was then on to a gig at Penzance which was another holiday camp for one night. This was a great earner for us and had nothing to do with music. We liked a game of snooker so we popped in to the camp's snooker hall. The hall had been taken over by a bunch of holidaymakers in their twenties from Scotland. The snooker hall manager said they were in there every day and they were a pain in the arse. They were full of themselves and were taking on all-comers for money, against camp regulations. One of them was a really good player so we didn't get involved.

Later in the day we went into town and into the Temperance snooker hall for a game. On the next table to us a woman who must have been in her sixties was having a game. She was potting for fun, she was shit hot. When she came off the table I said to her:

'Where'd you learn to play like that?'

'I used to teach people snooker back in Sunderland. I still keep my hand in. The blokes don't like playing against me as I normally beat them.'

She could give champion Fred Davis a run for his money. As they say up north she was a canny player. My mind was now racing in overdrive as I said to her:

'Do you want to earn some money?'

'Tell me more.'

Her name was Olga and I told her my plan. She was well up for it. We were going to take on the Jocks.

We arrived back at the camp and smuggled Olga in. It was straight into the snooker hall where we waited for a table next to the Jocks. When one became available Olga and I started playing, making sure that we were playing crap. The table next to us was where the main man was playing. Olga took a shot and made sure the red ball went off our table and went under his table. He got arsey and made it quite clear with four-letter words that women shouldn't be playing snooker.

With that Olga suggested he put his money where his mouth was and played a frame for a wager. The guy couldn't believe his luck, took a wedge of cash out of his back pocket and threw it on to the table. We'd already given Olga some funds to take him on and she matched his stake.

She wiped the floor with him. He just couldn't believe a sixty-year-old woman had thrashed him. She collected her winnings and we divvied up outside, giving us some welcome beer money.

୬ ୬ ୬

Next we played Camborne, followed by Newquay and our last gig on the tour was Ilfracombe in Devon.

As I've said, Billy was a wind-up merchant and he done me up like a kipper at Ilfracombe. I had a quick wash in the B&B before going on stage; he'd switched the bar of soap to a joke one. I played the whole gig with a black face.

As we made our way home decisions had to be made. Billy's drumming had calmed down and he'd settled in well. It was agreed he'd do Amsterdam and we'd see where that led us. We still had the issue with Rick who wanted to come back on board as our singer, a major problem.

We were, of course, still waiting to hear from the record company. High on the priority list was a professional manager to take us forward in a highly competitive industry. Anthony was still getting us some good-quality gigs so there was still plenty of work coming in.

♪ 22 ♪

Double Shuffle

We're off to Holland in three day's time so we have some time on our hands. Ray and Billy have gone back to Barnet and we're going to pick them up, plus Billy's drum kit, for the journey to the ferry terminal at Harwich. Anthony's been in touch to tell us the gig will now be two nights; ticket demand has gone through the roof, which is great news.

Being away so much we have no birds to come home to, so we ring Mandy and Viv to see if we can meet up. They blow us out as they now have a couple of guys in tow. So it's down to the double shuffle for Steve and me.

It works like this. First of all you put your smart gear on and make yourself look like the dog's bollocks. A splash of Old Spice and you're ready for the pull. We drive into Hornchurch and head for the shopping centre. Then it's into one of the big department stores, ladies fashion department. Leonards is our first port of call; we find the department we want, and I go in first, while Steve has a coffee.

You look for a girl assistant about your age to serve you and then you start giving it the spiel, making sure you don't sound too common, not easy for me.

'Hi, I'm looking for one of these new type of suede jackets for my sister's birthday, do you know what I mean?'

'Yeah, they've just come in, come this way I'll show you.'

'Sorry, what's your name?'

'Liz.'

'Thanks Liz, I'll follow you then.'

On reaching the rack of suede jackets she says:

'Do you know her size?'

'That's the problem I don't, but looking at your nice figure, you'll be about the same size.'

Then you look for the signs, they either blush when you talk about nice figures or they give you that old-fashioned piss-off look. She's the blushing type.

'Liz, as you're about the same size as my sister would you mind putting on the green one to see what it looks like.'

She looks slightly embarrassed as she puts the coat on. I take a step back and using the wow factor, say:

'I hope you don't mind me saying it, but that looks fantastic on you. You should get your boyfriend to buy you one.'

This is crunch time as you now find out whether she has a boyfriend.

'I haven't got a boyfriend at the moment.'

You don't follow that up straight away; you change the subject.

'My sister will love this. I'll find out what colour she'd like, I've got to get it before I go on tour.'

It's now a golden silence job as hopefully she asks the right question, which shouldn't take long. We're in business when she says,

'What type of tour are you going on?'

'I play in a band and we're off to a gig in Holland.'

You don't say any more about the band and you leave her with her thoughts. You give it a few seconds and leave adding:

'Thanks for all your help, Liz, you've been great. I'll find out the colour and be back.'

It's time to share a coffee with Steve for ten minutes then go back to the shop and Liz. You wait till she's not serving anybody and go over to her; hopefully, she's pleased to see you.

'Liz, I hope you don't mind me asking you. I'm going to the Sombrero coffee bar in Upminster tonight. I wonder if you'd like to have a coffee with me?'

Of course she's not expecting this so not too heavy with the chat.

'I don't even know your name?'

'It's Nick, and it's only a coffee, I could meet you there?'

'I'm meeting my friend Sandra tonight.'

'That's okay I can bring my mate Steve along. He plays in the same band as me.'

'What's your band's name?'

'Modern Edge.'

That hit the right note, a big smile appeared.

'I've heard of you.'

'Yeah, we've made some records, toured with a few big-name groups. Look I'd better go now, sorry I bothered you.'

I turn away and leave, hoping there's a response. I'm not disappointed.

'Nick, I wouldn't normally do this but we live in Cranham and the Sombrero is just round the corner to us.'

'That's great, Liz, about 7.00 if that fits in with you and Sandra?'

'Okay, Nick, see you there tonight.'

I meet up with Steve and tell him he won't have to do a double shuffle today. I was lucky; sometimes it takes three or four different shops before you get a result.

'What do you mean I ain't got a double shuffle?'

'She's got a mate called Sandra.'

'Oh no, not one of your blind dates again.'

'If she looks like Liz you'll be well pleased.'

'Nick, do you remember the last blind date you lumbered me with? The bible basher, the one with the liberty bodice and thick tights, there was no chance of a leg over there. What with the bad breath, goofy teeth and a nose so big it covered all her face, what a blinding night that was.'

೭ು ೭ು ೭ು

We put the radio on as we make our way to the coffee bar in Steve's Vauxhall Velox, complete with column gears. One of the news items is that the government has made pirate radio stations illegal using the Marine Offences Act. This means goodbye to Radio Caroline and Radio London, a real blow. Our first record had been played on a pirate radio station and these stations were a big help in promoting new records for bands.

We go into the Sombrero. We've played in there when we first started up. There are no girls waiting for us so I get the coffees in. After the second Woodbine doubts are kicking in as to whether we're being blown out. The coffee bar is nearly empty as there's a dance over the road in the Windmill, nicknamed 'The Shelter' because it's like a long air-raid shelter. It's a good venue and there's always a lot of talent on show.

We're just about to leave when the girls come in. Liz looks great in her red hot pants and I'm hoping for a good night. Sandra isn't bad at all. It helps that she does have a pair on her, they looked deformed. The white button top she wears is certainly taking the strain; I can't see the buttons lasting very long before they pop. Steve is happy and Sandra seems to like him. Liz and I hit it off straight away so everything is fine.

Tonight we'd planned to go over to the Windmill and have a dance. The girls are up for that so we pay our 3/6d and go in. We must like them as we pay for them as well, which is a first. There's a poster at the entrance advertising the band's name; they are called The Bosticks, which I haven't heard of before. As we enter The Shelter they're playing 'Barbara Ann' by the Beach Boys. The lads are in their early teens and sound all right.

The four of us have a good night and the old twisting shoes are on top form. As the band plays 'No Milk Today' by Herman's Hermits I quickly pull Liz towards me and hold her as close as I can. She doesn't object and her Topaze perfume smells lovely as I nibble her ear and put my hand on her bum. Steve has a problem dancing with Sandra. Her tits are so big he can't get close enough to her.

After the dance we stop off for a snog in a nearby field. Steve makes it quite clear that the motor is his and I have to get out. As it's a warm evening I don't have a problem with that so Liz and I find a nice spot near the motor. We both laugh when we heard Sandra shout out:

'Look, Steve, I'm not like that.'

It appears Steve won't take no for an answer when Sandra continues:

'Steve, stop putting your hand down there, will you.'

This is putting me off my stroke. I wish they'd put the windows up, it's like a bleedin' scene from *Peyton Place*.

Quiet prevails as Liz and I are on the last lap, only to be interrupted again with a loud shout from Steve:

'I've got feckin' cramp, it's killing me.'

It all goes downhill after that as he won't stop bleating about his leg. I see Liz for the next two nights; she's a really nice girl. I'm thinking to myself perhaps there's a little bit of courting coming on; the problem is that we're off to Amsterdam so anything could happen there.

♪ 23 ♪

Amsterdam

As the four of us made our way to Harwich for the Amsterdam gig, there was one burning question, which one of us was going to drive on the right-hand side of the road when we got there? I didn't fancy it and Steve has trouble driving in this country. Ray said no way, leaving Billy whose driving was like his drumming, fast and furious with a few bumps on the way.

We arrived at Harwich for the ten-hour ferry trip to the Hook of Holland. Once we were on the ferry, still in one piece after Billy's driving, we were thinking about the gig. We were playing at a theatre in the centre of Amsterdam and didn't know what to expect; they were even putting us up in a hotel next to the theatre. We were looking forward to a new adventure for the group, albeit with only two of the original members.

The crossing was fair, helped by plenty of cheap booze. On arrival Billy got in the driver's seat again and drove to our hotel in Amsterdam or so we thought. After about ten miles we found out we were going the wrong way and had to turn around. Looking out of the window we noticed there were more windmills out there than pubs down the Old Kent Road.

We drove into the car park after scraping a post that had suddenly moved towards us! The young attendant said in perfect English:

'We've been waiting for you and so have they.'

Suddenly about a dozen girls rushed over asking for autographs. We were overwhelmed by all the attention we were getting, surely we weren't that well known in Holland?

We were playing the following night so the rest of the day was for sightseeing. The hotel rooms were the best we'd ever stayed in. A meal was laid on and the younger members of the hotel staff were continually telling us that they were coming to the gigs. We were being treated like some mega band and we enjoyed the attention.

We went to the theatre next door to give it the once over. It was big, in fact it was more than big, it was massive. Arses were twitching as I looked at Billy and Ray. They were used to playing to a hundred or two, but this was big time. There was a hoarding above the entrance. I could make out Modern Edge; the rest was all double Dutch to me! We asked someone walking by what it said:

'Come and see the number one Mod band from England, Modern Edge.'

I thought why did we need a manager. Anthony was doing a great job promoting us, so why waste our money?

We went into the foyer and were greeted by a girl who I can only describe as gorgeous.

'Hi. I'm Steve from the band, we're playing here tomorrow. Sorry, what's your name?'

With a nice smile she replied:

'Tryne. If you'd like to hang on a minute I'll get the manager for you, Steve.'

'Bleedin' hell, Steve you were quick off the mark,' I said.

'The way she said Steve made everything turn to jelly.'

'Not everything,' piped up Ray with a laugh.

A guy of about 30 with whitish hair and dressed in a smart suit came over to us, who was Tryne's husband, unfortunately for Steve.

'Hi guys, my name's Van, great to have you here, I'll take you through to the theatre.'

It was mind-boggling, what a place. It had two tiers and there were hundreds of seats covered in red plush brocade.

He was telling us who had played there before, all household names. We felt a bit of a fraud as we were really a nothing band compared with them. He said that the two nights were sold out and that every Mod in Amsterdam wanted to come. He added that our record was still being played regularly over the airwaves and that had drummed up a lot of interest. What really annoyed Steve and me was why had our last record company kicked us into touch, when we could fill a venue like this in Holland, it didn't make sense.

We'd arranged with Van that we'd set up early the following morning because we wanted to rehearse all day. We really had to be on top form for the two nights. Billy still had work to do on the numbers we'd written; it wasn't his fault as he'd come to us on the hoof. On the covers he was fine, mind you we'd have to book up for hearing aids when we got back home!

I must admit we were all well nervous about the gigs so what was the answer for four innocent young lads – the red light district.

20 20 20

After showering, the Old Spice went on and we're ready for a journey into the unknown. Billy preferred British Sterling after shave; you could smell that a bleedin' mile away. The Woodbines are lit and we're on a roll. Ray asks the hotel doorman which is the best district to go to.

'De Wallen, that's where it all hangs out', he tells us.

We jump into a cab for the 20-minute journey – that's the first rip-off of the night when we find out it's only a two-minute walk from the hotel. The four of us have been to Soho and we think that's a bit naughty but this is something else. To say it is in your face is an understatement. There are birds sitting in shop windows offering all sorts of goodies. I've never paid for it, so that isn't going to change. I can't get my head around it. I suppose it's a bit more exciting than going into your local shop for the *Daily Mirror* and a packet of Players Weights.

Billy has no problem paying for it and he has us walking up and down the street eyeing up shop windows to see which one he fancies. He decides on this girl with olive skin. Before he goes in he says:

'D'yer reckon she'll have a Johnnie?'

'If she ain't,' says Ray, 'you'll be down the clap clinic tomorrow.'

He disappears into the doorway and comes back straight away.

'I ain't got enough guilders on me, can anybody sub me?'

So there we are, having a whip round for a bunk-up.

He goes back in, the curtain's closed and he's up and running. Within ten minutes he's out again with a big grin on his face.

'How was it, then?' says Ray.

He thinks for a moment and then says.

'It was like driving through Blackwall Tunnel on a wet night.'

'Sounds really nice!' says Ray. 'At least it's the first foreign bird you've scored with Billy.'

'I thought so too, until she opened her gob.'

'What do you mean?'

'She's from Liverpool.'

We all have a good laugh on the strength of that and then a few beers in one of the bars. As we come out of the bar there's a bloke wearing a long leather jacket outside a club shouting out:

'Live fecky' fecky.'

We look at each other and think we're having some of that. We pay the entrance fee and go into this dark room with a stage; the room has about 50 seats in it. There's a full house and we're ready for the action. Looking around there are a few likely lads like us, some others with long coats on who look a bit pervy, and, amazingly, some girls. Suddenly Tchaikovsky's 1812 overture thunders out making us jump out of our skin. This bloke of about 30 with an athletic body, appears on the stage with just his boxers on. Then a girl in her early twenties, who's got the full kit on, saunters over to him.

The music goes up another few decibels and our eyes pop out of our head. The guy drops his boxers and there's this thing hanging there. Steve shouts out:

'Christ, look at the size of that hampton?'

The four of us look down below and Ray mutters:

'He's got more than all the rest of us put together.'

Then the girl whips her black lacy knickers off and then, well I've never seen anything like it. The music is still pounding while he's giving her one at every imaginable angle and more. It's unreal and takes sex to another level. Giving your bird one in the back of a Ford Cortina will never be the same. This goes on for about 20 minutes until the final crescendo, which I won't go into. All I'll say, it was a bit iffy even by our standards.

We make our way out of the club, shaking our heads in disbelief. It's time to go back to the hotel and we walk this time.

We pass Billy's girl in the shop window. She's still there smiling and wobbling her tits about. Billy waves to her and she lifts her right hand up and bends her little finger. We roar with laughter as Ray calls out:

'See she was impressed with you then, Billy boy.'

༄ ༄ ༄

The next morning it was back to the business end as we set the gear up on stage for a full day of rehearsing. The sound engineer and the lighting guy were very helpful, making sure everything was going to be all right on the night. This was a proper gig and the nerves were starting to kick in. We worked really hard and were pleased with the results. Billy had now come into line with his drumming and he was starting to grow on us. The only problem he had was some itching down below; of course all the jokes came out. Ray was wicked as he kept winding him up.

'Them crabs on the move already, Billy.'

'You can't get crabs that quick, can you Ray?'

While the banter was in full flow we noticed people coming in with TV cameras and other equipment. We didn't think anything more of it until we stopped for a break. Van came over and said he liked what he was hearing. I stopped him in his tracks and said:

'What's with all the cameras?'

'That's for tonight, Nick.'

'I'm not with you, Van.'

He looked at all four of us and said:

'You don't know, do you?'

'Know what?' I replied.

'Didn't Anthony talk to you?'

'About what?'

'Have you ever appeared on television?'

'I wish,' I said.

'Well you are now. This company is making a film about Mods and Rockers in England. And with you in town and being top of the Mod bands they felt your music would enhance the film. They're going to film the whole gig and then use what they want.'

'I don't believe it,' said Steve.

He immediately phoned his dad and asked him what was going on. It wasn't that we minded, but it would've been nice to know about it and secondly to know what was in it for us.

Later he rang back. Anthony had sent a telex to him at the solicitors where he worked to advise him of the film company, but somehow it never reached him. It was a good earner for us. What it did tell us is that we couldn't run *ad hoc* anymore. No disrespect to Tom but we needed a full-time manager looking after our affairs.

Later on in the day it was the news we'd all been waiting for. Tom phoned to say that the record company had got in touch and we had an appointment with John H. Fitzgerald on our return. To say we were excited was an understatement; it felt like all our birthdays had come at once. But there's a saying, it doesn't happen until 'The Fat Lady Sings'.

The person producing the film was English. Richard was a great guy and put us at ease about it. He was out of Bow in East London. He said the film was for the Dutch and European market, including being shown on English television in about six weeks' time. All the other parts of the film had been completed; our bit would be the last to be canned.

'I hope you realise that this film will be seen in the homes of tens of thousands of people. The coverage could take you to another level.'

After Richard's comments we had a band meeting. We realised that we had to play at least one or possibly two more of our own numbers, if we were going to be on the box.

'It would be great for the viewers to hear our original numbers,' I said.

'I'm worried, guys, I don't want to let you down. I'm still not sure about some of your own material.'

'Look Billy,' I said. 'You've helped us out of trouble when we didn't have a drummer and we respect that. We've got another five hours of rehearsing, what we'll do is to go over our own numbers again and again. You'll be great. mate.'

Steve butted in and added:

'Billy, it's not the drumming we're worried about, it's you scratching your feckin' nuts on camera.'

ॐ ॐ ॐ

We'd finished the practising and were now in the dressing room getting ourselves togged up. It was agreed that as it was a Mod night we'd put on our target tee-shirts for the first set and our union jack ones for the second set. With our Lee Cooper jeans, pork pie hats and baseball boots we did look the part.

Van came in with the lovely Tryne and wished us luck. The theatre was full, the cameras were ready to roll and we were shitting ourselves. The Woodbines came out plus a few Dutch beers to give us some Dutch courage!

'Okay, lads, let's get the show on the road,' I said.

We shook hands with each other and walked on to the stage. The reception we got from the crowd was overwhelming. We plugged in and the four of us looked at each other, we knew it wouldn't get any better than this and went straight into 'Suburban Mod'.

The two nights went well; Richard was pleased with the filming and he was going to send us a copy. He'd let us know when it was going to be televised in England. The Dutch teenagers certainly liked our music and it was a shame we couldn't get it together with any of them. But we had more important things on our mind than girls.

Before we got back on the ferry we loaded up with duty free. We had more booze and fags than the local Off Licence back in Essex. It was an optimistic trip back to Harwich with our thoughts of a record deal and possibly becoming a major player in the pop world.

♪ 24 ♪

All that Glisters is not Gold

When I got home there was the usual crap. My brother Arthur was now an apprentice electrician. From being a chef where he poisoned most of the customers, he's now going to feckin' electrocute them. He still had that dopey bird Deirdre in tow. Because my mum was a lot better dad was now back up the Legion six nights a week. That wasn't on and I had a quiet word with him to tell him to get his priorities right. He said:

'You're right, Nick, instead of taking mum up the Legion one night I'll make it two!'

As I was tucking into homemade sausage toad, chips and beans, mum said:

'While you were away, that lovely Anita rang me again to see how I was. She's a smashing girl you know, you'd do well to marry a girl like that, rather than knock around with all them 'Good Time Girls'.'

Her comment about good time girls made me laugh, so much so a chip caught down my throat making me choke. She does come up with some right gems.

'Yeah, I know she's a nice girl mum, but she's promised to somebody else.'

'That might be so, Nick, but take it from someone who's been taken off the shelf a few times and dusted down, she still cares about you.'

Another chip went down the wrong way when she said that.

🐦 🐦 🐦

Steve, Tom and I caught the train from Romford to Liverpool Street and then the Circle line to Euston Square for our meeting with John H. Fitzgerald at the record company's office. Ray felt that it would be best if Steve and I represented the band. Billy was now working on a month to month basis, which suited both parties.

We felt in a buoyant mood as we waited in reception for John H. as we now called him. There were plenty of gold discs and photos of bands represented by the company; many were well-known faces. We had a cup of coffee and were waiting to go in. We heard John H. on the intercom say:

'Send them in.'

He greeted us and after a quick chitchat it was straight down to the nitty gritty.

'Okay, lads, this is where we are. We're interested in signing you up. We had somebody in Holland watching you over the weekend and they were impressed. That's the good news.'

'Don't tell me there's bad news, Mr. Fitzgerald?' I sighed.

He picked up a document from the table and said:

'I'm afraid there is. Your previous company have a clause in the contract stating that your band cannot record with another company for a year.'

'What!'

'I'm sorry, Nick, that's how it is.'

'But they made it quite clear they didn't want us anymore.'

'That's as maybe, but they won't shift. I've spoken to their director, he was adamant on his decision. They did say that if we paid them a fee they would release you from the contract. The money they were asking for is not in our budget so I'm afraid it's no go at the moment.'

'Where does that leave us, then?'

'Well, Nick, it's like this. If you can't put this to bed with your previous company in the next few weeks we will withdraw our interest in you. You have to remember the pop world changes weekly. At the moment your music and band are flavour of the month but next month it could be a different ball game. I'll give you some advice, whoever managed you before didn't have a clue. He or she should've checked the fine print, because they've let you down badly. Whoever you get next time to manage the band make sure they fully understand this business otherwise you're going to get ripped off again.'

'Rick's dad was a right bastard,' said a very angry Steve.

'Sorry, lads that's it. We'll keep in touch but you've got to find a way for them to release you and quickly, best of luck.'

Where do we Go from Here?

After the bad news from John H. Fitzgerald, Steve, Tom and I went straight back to my house to plot the next move. Ray and Billy were going to meet us there. Fortunately we had local gigs in the next couple of weeks so there was no travelling which was a blessing.

While we were all there I phoned up Johnny Curtis, the weasel from the previous record company, and asked the question, why are you holding us to ransom when you don't want us to record with you anymore? Smarmy and condescending, and lying through his teeth, he said it was nothing to do with him. The final decision was with his American boss, J. Rivera, who we'd had a fall out with. He was adamant he wouldn't change his mind.

We were well and truly stuffed and we didn't know what to do next. Tom was going to get one of the partners at the solicitors he worked for to have a look at the contract to see if there were any loopholes.

Later we were all having a chat when there was a knock on the door. Standing there was Ronnie, who looked well spived up with his crombie, gold chains and dark glasses on.

'Nick, my son, get the kettle on, I'm parched.'

He had an irritating habit of pouring his tea into a saucer and slurping from it.

'What's new then, Ronnie?'

'I'm onto something, big Steve, and as you're my mates. I'm going to let you into a little secret.'

'Don't worry, Ronnie,' I said, 'you keep your secret. There's always a catch.'

'Look this is ridgey didge. I'm on a right good earner and I'm going to share it with you.'

'Ronnie, you don't even share a cold.'

'Nick, listen to what I've got to say. A mate of mine works at this stockbrokers in the City of London and he's got some right good info.'

'Keep it to yourself, this will cost us money,' I said.

'Just listen, he's told me there's an oil share that's going to move up the charts and there's a lot of quick money to be made. At present this share is at a low price, but within a week or two you can at least treble your money. It's that good I've bought some already.'

So moving on a little, what did we do? We laid out some hard-earned cash, as did all our mates at La Nero. We gave the money to Steve's dad who knew all about these things and he bought some shares on our behalf. Unfortunately for him he had a flutter as well. For the first couple of days they shot up, then the inevitable happened, they crashed to near enough zero. When we finally found Ronnie, who was holed up with his brother in Scotland away from all the flack, I said to him:

'Ronnie, what was your mate's job in this stockbroker's office?'

'Well, it's like this. He didn't actually work for them as such. He's an electrician and while he was putting some sockets in their office, he heard this rumour about this oil share!'

❧ ❧ ❧

As Ray and Billy left my house after our meeting we arranged to pick them up the following day for the next gig, which was one we weren't looking forward to. It was in Stratford, East London. The pub we were playing at was a rough house; if the punters didn't like the band they let you know with their fists.

Later that night Rick phoned and I have to be honest I wasn't that friendly. Rick wanted to see us so Steve and I reluctantly went round to his drum. He was full of the joys of spring. He couldn't get his words out quick enough:

'The sale for dad's transport business should go through in the next four weeks, so get the mic ready for my comeback.'

Rather awkwardly I replied:

'There's a lot of water gone under the bridge since you left the band.'

Rick got arsey and spat his words out:

'What do you mean by that? It was agreed that I would come back on board once I'd sorted out the old man's affairs.'

Steve lost it:

'Don't talk to me about your old man, Rick, he's thieved from us, he's lied to us and now he's cost us a new record deal. He never showed that contract to any solicitor otherwise they'd have pointed out what a crap deal it was.'

Rick was gobsmacked. Perhaps Steve shouldn't have said what he said, but he had. In fairness, we've got eyes as well, and perhaps the four of us should've paid more attention to the fine details of the contract.

We explained to a now subdued Rick about the new record company and what had been said about our previous contract. We tried to say that it wasn't because of that that we didn't want him back in the band, but there were issues that needed to be sorted. The truth was that Ray was an asset to the band and we didn't want to get rid of him. But Rick was one of the founder members and we had said we'd welcome him back when he was ready; we were now backtracking.

We left Rick, not on the best of terms and said that when the sale of the business had gone through we would talk again.

We headed for La Nero; we always seemed to go there when we had issues with the band. I suppose that is where we started and it felt right to be there to discuss our next move. Ted still ran the coffee bar and brought over a couple of chocolate milk shakes and two large cream slices.

'How's the group going, lads?' he asked. 'You're still Romford's number one band, then.'

'I don't know about that, Ted,' said Steve. 'It's a bit of a dog's dinner at the moment.'

'How are Rick and Tony?'

'How long have you got,' replied Steve.

'It's like that then, lads, is it?'

'I'm afraid it is mate, how's life with you?'

'Bit tough at the moment, Nick, there's coffee bars springing up everywhere, so business could be better. I need to revamp the place and get it back on the map.'

'Maybe we could do a gig for you on the house,' I said. 'We'll come back to you and work out a date.'

≈ ≈ ≈

The following day we picked up Ray before going to Stratford, and said we'd spoken to Rick. We made it clear to Ray that he was part of the band and whatever happened to the line-up he was here to stay, which put his mind at rest.

We then picked up Billy and he indicated to us that a mate in a well-known heavy rock band could be looking for a drummer for a tour of the USA soon.

It didn't get any better that night. It wasn't the music they didn't like, it was each other, what a punch-up. As I was hiding, trying to protect the gear, I thought to myself it was a bit different from Amsterdam.

We were plodding from one gig to another and still making a living so we couldn't complain. Rick made contact, his dad had said he was really sorry he'd messed up and he'd make amends for all the grief he'd put us through. How he was going to accomplish that doing a three-year stretch in one of Her Majesty's, I don't know. We were at least on speaking terms with Rick now.

Richard from the film company sent us a tape of the gig in Amsterdam, but it was no use to us because we didn't have a film projector. He confirmed that it would be on television in two weeks' time so we'd see it then.

꘎ ꘎ ꘎

As we had a couple of days off we'd taken the Transit to Des's to have some work done. Then we had a panic call from our agent:

'Nick, can you help, one of my bands have let me down for a two-night gig in Corby, starting tomorrow.'

It was good money so I quickly phoned the other guys and they were up for it. One problem, we didn't have a van so we were going to have to hire one. The only vehicle we could get at short notice was a small minibus which had seats in. So we hired this out and took it around to Steve's dad's garage at the back of his house. The garage was full of spare parts of Steve's old motors which had been discarded. Steve and I spent the whole morning taking all the seats out so that we could put our amps and the rest of the gear in the back of it.

We did the Corby gigs which went down well and made our way back home. As we arrived late we decided to put the seats back in first thing in the morning.

As we opened the front of the garage the next morning we stood there in amazement. It was like a new pin, all the old auto parts and the seats from the minibus were gone. Panic set in as Steve went into his house and rang his dad up at work. Within a couple of minutes he was back and said:

'You won't believe it. While we were away the old man decided it was a great opportunity to have a clear out when this rag and bone man knocked on his door. The bloke must have thought it was Christmas, he took everything including the seats.'

'Tell me you're joking.'

'I wish I was. There's a family of tinkers right now sitting around their camp fire in some nice new seats.'

After that it was thinking on your feet time. We took the minibus back to the rental company one minute before closing time. As we walked in, the lad was more concerned in getting home. As I gave him back the keys he said:

'Just park it around the back, mate.'

Tongue in cheek I said:

'Don't you want to check it first?'

'No I've got a bird to meet. Just put it round the back in the yard with the others.'

We were out of that office in seconds and parked it up against a fence which backed on to a field. We then pulled a bit of the chain link fence down between the field and the yard. The idea was that when the shit hit the fan they might think some likely lads had broken in and nicked the seats.

Of course they did get in touch and our answer was:

'Not us, guv.'

♪ 26 ♪

The Fat Lady Sings

The next month was going to be interesting to say the least. It started off with Billy telling us that he was joining the rock band, so again we were looking for a drummer.

Rick came back to us and said his dad was on the case regarding the contract of our previous company and we should be getting a letter soon from them. We didn't take much notice about that, it sounded like a load of old tosh.

It was the evening of the film. The four of us were round my house in front of the black and white Bush television devouring the last of our Amsterdam duty frees. We couldn't believe our eyes. The film started with Mods and Rockers knocking shit out of each other at Brighton back in the mid sixties. It then progressed to examining why the youth of today in Britain was more rebellious than in any other generation. It went on to say how the sixties music scene would probably be known as the decade that changed the world of modern music forever.

Then it was us, what a magic feeling watching yourself on the telly. We'd always wanted to play on television, and it was for a whole ten minutes. What a great buzz that was. Then we all burst out laughing when the camera panned on Billy for a few seconds, and there he was having a quick scratch of his nuts.

We were totally mesmerised. You can always find fault in your performance but I have to say I thought we were on top of our game.

When the film finished the phone didn't stop ringing, even Anita rang to say congratulations.

❧ ❧ ❧

The next day I woke up with a mega hangover and suffering from tobacco poisoning. Waking up in the morning still pissed was going to be a major problem in a couple of weeks' time for the band. One of us always had to drive to the next gig still under the influence, with a fair amount of alcohol in our system. We'd have to look at this now as the government was launching a breathalyser test for drivers. If I'd blown into a bag then I'd have bleedin' burst it. Even though it was going to cramp our lifestyle it made sense as being drunk and killing people was not an option. We would in future make sure one of the band members was drink-free when driving the gig van.

I was just lighting my second smoke of the day when there was a knock on the door. The postman was standing there and asked:

'Are you Mr. N. Sheldon?'

'That's me.'

He gave me a recorded letter which I signed for. My eyes were so blurred I had to have a cup of tea before I read it. With a ciggy on the go I opened the official-looking envelope and read the contents.

The letter was mind-boggling. Our previous record company had written to say they'd cancelled our contract and we were free to pursue whatever avenues we wished. Later on that day I got a call from John H. He'd had a copy of this letter, too, and was delighted that this unfortunate episode had been sorted out. It was agreed that we'd see each other in a week's time; he couldn't do it any quicker as he had to fly out to Spain for a few days. He was very impressed with our performance on television and said that the show would only enhance our popularity.

I don't know even today how Rick's dad pulled it off. I have my own ideas but I'll keep them to myself.

ॐ ॐ ॐ

Gigs still had to be honoured and this weekend we were back in Reading working for T.J. He welcomed us with open arms and went overboard about the film. He also made it clear that he would like to manage us and had put a business plan together if we still wanted him. We knew he was a shrewd operator and he'd always been straight with us. Even better, the company who owned the complex and others around the country were expanding into band management. Instead of going through agents they were cutting out the middle man. With their own stable of groups, they would now be the agents and find work for the bands that were coming on board with them. They were a big outfit and T.J. was heading up this new venture; it sounded just what we wanted. We were to become the first band on board with this new company.

ॐ ॐ ॐ

There was also another first in the same month which would help bands like us to promote their records. The BBC was launching Radio 1, a music station aimed at a younger audience. This was taking over from the pirate radio stations which had now been banned. Mind you, some of the disc jockeys had previously been working on the boats. They included Dave Cash, Ed Stewart, Pete Drummond, John Peel and Tony Blackburn, who opened up the station with 'Flowers In The Rain' by The Move. Hopefully in the weeks to come our record label could get our records played on the new station.

❧ ❧ ❧

It was another sell-out night, and we were up for it. Girls had been put on the back burner for the last couple of weeks so we had to remedy that. I wasn't expecting Anita to show, but even if she did we knew it wasn't going anywhere so I was on the prowl for some female company.

About an hour before going on stage we went into the bar to see what was on offer. Who should be there but none other than Anita, Jenny and the rest of the girls from the salon. They came over to us straightaway. It appeared Anita was pleased to see me, which was a bonus. We could only stay a few minutes as we had to complete the last sound check but I quickly took her away from the rest of her girls and said:

'Perhaps I can see you after the show?'

'Okay, Nick, maybe we should have a chat to clear up a few things. I'll tell you what, I'll meet you outside the stage door after the gig.'

'Yeah, I'll be there.'

Steve, Ray and Billy were going to a club with girls from the salon after the show.

When things are going well you sometimes get a bit sloppy when you play, but it wasn't going to happen to us. We hadn't signed the deal yet so we had to be on our mettle. It was a good night and we all had something to look forward to after the gig!

☙ ☙ ☙

I met Anita by the stage door and we jumped into her Mini and drove off. I had to ask the question:

'Where're we going?'

'Back to my flat, but don't get any ideas, Nick, this is purely platonic. Simon and I are well known in the town and I don't want any tittle tattle from anyone.'

'Where's The Saint, Simon Templar, tonight then?'

'Don't be facetious, Nick, it doesn't suit you.'

I was saying to myself what does that mean, so I just said: 'Sorry.'

'He's playing in a National Cup rugby match up in Lancashire.'

'What if he comes home now?'

'He doesn't live with me, Nick.'

'Oh.'

I felt like a naughty little boy who should only speak when he was spoken to. Here was a girl who had her own thriving business and a motor, her boyfriend's a well-known athlete and high flyer, and there was me with my arse hanging out of my strides and smoking Woodbines.

We finally arrived at a two-storey block of flats in a nice area. She opened the door to her flat, what a pad. It was so posh I took my baseball boots off, revealing two bleedin' big holes in my white socks. Anita looked at me and laughed. I had to say something:

'You're making me feel like a right peasant, can't we go back to that innocent Anita I met in Dawlish a few years back?'

She seemed shocked and said:

'What do mean by that, Nick?'

'It's only that you seem to be in business mode all the time, always on your guard.'

'With you, I have to be. Let's be honest, Nick, you and that band of yours chase more girls in a month than most blokes do in a lifetime. Do you know what the girls call your band in the salon?'

'Something nice, I hope.'

'Rampant rabbits.'

'How did they come up with that?'

'Because you're always burrowing for holes.'

I looked at her in disbelief.

'I can't believe you said that, Anita.'

'Nor can I.'

We both burst out laughing and couldn't stop.

She made coffee and walked over to the new Dansette which sat on four legs, unlike mine, just an old carry-case type. The first record was 'Sealed With A Kiss' by Brian Hyland.

'When I hear this record it reminds me of when I first met you,' I said.

'And me, Nick.'

It was just a pity that we couldn't take it any further, but that's how it was. After about an hour she hinted that it was time for me to go; I took the hint.

'I'll give you a lift back to the hotel, Nick.'

'I don't want you driving about in the middle of the night, I'll call a taxi.'

She tried to say it was all right but I was having none of it so she called a cab. As we waited by the front door I heard the taxi coming up the road. I kissed her on the cheek and gave her a quick cuddle. We both looked at each other and all the emotions of our up-and-down relationship over the last few years came out. We just held on to each other and didn't let go until Anita said:

'I don't want you to go, Nick.'

ව ව ව

Epilogue

We signed up with the record company and went straight into their studio. They listened to some of our own material but didn't think it was strong enough. They came up with a number for us which was a great move both on their behalf and for us, as the record went straight into the charts. We also later recorded an LP that also went really well.

It was a shrewd move getting T.J. on board. His company really looked after us and with his help it took the band on an unbelievable journey. We played some great venues to thousands of people. We travelled across Europe and beyond; unfortunately we didn't play the Hollywood Bowl!

Billy did leave the band, and is now riding high with his heavy London Rock 'n' Roll band.

We visited Penny to see whether Tony was coming back to England, as we badly needed a drummer. Bad news on that front, Tony had been arrested on a drugs charge and was now rotting in prison somewhere in the Far East. I suppose that was a lesson for us all, don't touch drugs.

As previously mentioned Penny was a drummer in her own right and had her own band. Their father was a drummer in the big bands of the forties and fifties and still played a bit. He'd taught both of them to play at an early age. Penny had played a few gigs for us before and we knew she could cut it. We offered her the job and after talking to her mum and dad she accepted. Girl drummers were nothing new in the sixties. The Honeycombs had Honey Lantree, also a good singer. They had that big hit in 1964 'Have I The Right'.

When we got back from Reading we met up with Rick and I'm pleased to say that he joined the band again on keyboards and vocals, which was really great news. Ray was now a permanent fixture in the band. So we were now a five-piece which enabled us to do so much more musically.

We went to visit Rick's dad in prison; he wanted to apologise personally to us. We weren't too sure about it, but felt it could put a few demons to rest. We didn't ask Rick's dad why the company had changed their mind so rapidly. That was his secret and we didn't want to know.

Talking about prisons, Des's luck ran out, he got banged up for a year, a combination of motoring offences and growing illegal herbal plants in his greenhouses. He was out in a few months and became our driver and one of our roadies. I'm pleased to say he has kept out of mischief, well we think he has. He was a handy bloke on your team as he got us out of trouble on many occasions when gig vans and amps were playing up – he can fix anything.

We did the free gig in La Nero. Ted helped us when we first started, so we owed him. Ronnie showed up at the gig, still wheeling and dealing, and tried to sell me a new Japanese colour television which he said was the first one in the country. I did have a look at it in the back of his Austin A40 van. On closer inspection I noticed a coloured piece of Perspex on the screen and said:

'Ronnie, do I look a bit divvy.'

'What do you expect for a tenner, Nick?'

Alec turned up with his bird. Last time I'd seen him he looked like he'd come from the Chelsea flower show with the clobber he had on. He'd gone back to being a Mod, and said with a laugh:

'All those flowers were giving me hay fever.'

He'd now got himself a new super-duper Lambretta with more lights on it than Blackpool seafront.

Anita finally broke up with her boyfriend. We were now seeing each other on a regular basis. With my lifestyle and track record we agreed to take it day by day. Her business went from strength to strength; she and Jenny had opened a second salon, with a third in the pipeline.

Steve got back together with Jenny as well, so when we went to see them we'd go up together.

Within three months I'd lost both my mum and dad. Dad had a heart attack down the Legion one Friday night and died there and then. If he was going to go I suppose down his favourite place with his mates around him was as good as place as any. He was only 48 and it had a devastating effect on my mum. A few weeks later she sadly passed away. She was heartbroken by dad's death and this must have played some part in her having a fatal stroke.

When both your parents die within a short period it takes the stuffing out of you and it's hard to keep it all together. I did have my mates in the band to lean on, which really helped my grief.

My brother Arthur couldn't take it on board at all and he was totally wiped out about what had happened to the family unit; to be fair we all were. He and Deirdre then decided on the spur of the moment that they were going to travel round the world and left the country. I haven't heard from him since.

Living in your family home on your own at 21 years of age with all the photos and memories of happier days around you is hard to take.

At my mum's funeral we played her favourite record, Billy Fury's 'Half Way To Paradise' which was unheard of in those days. As we laid her to rest I thought of all the struggles she'd had to ensure that we didn't go without.

I always smile when I recall her saying to me after returning from a late night gig, still pissed and puking everywhere with a Woodbine dangling out of my mouth:

'Nicholas, do you think this Rock 'n' Roll life is for you?'